Contents

CW00410959

Text copyright © BRF 2013
Authors retain copyright in their own work

Published by
The Bible Reading Fellowship
15 The Chambers
Abingdon, OX14 3FE
United Kingdom
Tel: +44 (0)1865 319700
Email: enquiries@brf.org.uk
Website: www.brf.org.uk
BRF is a Registered Charity

ISBN 978 0 85746 096 7
First published 2013
10 9 8 7 6 5 4 3 2 1 0

Acknowledgments
Scripture quotations taken from The Holy Bible, New International Version Copyright (Anglicised edition) copyright © 1973, 1978, 1984, 2011 by Biblica (formerly International Bible Society). Used by permission of Hodder & Stoughton Publishers, an Hachette UK company. All rights reserved. 'NIV' is a registered trade mark of Biblica (formerly International Bible Society). UK trademark number 1448790.

Scripture quotations taken from The Holy Bible, New International Version, copyright © 1973, 1978, 1984 by Biblica (formerly International Bible Society), are used by permission of Hodder & Stoughton, an Hachette UK company. All rights reserved. 'NIV' is a registered trademark of Biblica (formerly International Bible Society). UK trademark number 1448790.

Scripture quotations taken from The New Revised Standard Version of the Bible, Anglicised Edition, copyright © 1989, 1995 by the Division of Christian Education of the National Council of the Churches of Christ in the USA, and are used by permission. All rights reserved.

Scripture quotations from THE MESSAGE. Copyright © by Eugene H. Peterson 1993, 1994, 1995. Used by permission of NavPress Publishing Group.

Extracts from the Authorised Version of the Bible (The King James Bible), the rights in which are vested in the Crown, are reproduced by permission of the Crown's patentee, Cambridge University Press.

Extract from As a Child by Phil Steer, published by lulu.com, 2012; www.asachildbook.com

A catalogue record for this book is available from the British Library

Printed in Poland by Ozgraf

The Editor writes...

 Welcome to *Quiet Spaces*.

This issue covers an interesting time of year. We are just finishing summer, and by the end of the issue we will have experienced harvest, Advent, Christmas and New Year and will be in the middle of winter. We try to reflect on all these seasons in this issue and to bring some stillness and peace to these packed few months, as well as some challenge and learning.

In *Quiet Spaces* we try to provide permission to pray as suits you, to pray because you want to, not because you feel you ought to. Feel free to explore the styles of prayer on offer, be adventurous and try something you had never thought of and accept the gifts God gives from it; even if it is a struggle and the prayer feels dry, try reflecting on the experience and see where God was during your time of prayer. I also invite you to try praying for different lengths of time. Sometimes we have only a few minutes and at other times we may have half an hour or an hour, or even—luxury—half a day. Use the time you have available, not worrying about how short it might be. Recognise that we all have days when we struggle to manage any more than a few arrow prayers in the midst of the busyness.

I was challenged recently when someone asked if I saw prayer as homework, as something to be done that was set and had to be completed or I would get into trouble. For many of us prayer can become like that, a duty rather than a joy. I'm sure God does not intend time spent with him to be entered into other than from love for him and a desire to spend time with him. The desire to meet with him is the first step.

Remember that God delights in your friendship and longs to spend time with you. He cherishes the time you have together rather than bearing a grudge for the time you don't spend with him. So receive his forgiveness and turn to him.

Sally Smith

Writers in this issue

Helen Jaeger is the internationally published author of five books: *Paths Through Grief, As Night Falls, As Day Dawns, A Treasury of Wisdom* (Lion Hudson) and *Simple* (Scripture Union, 2003). She writes regularly for a variety of publications, including *Woman Alive* and for charities. Helen is also an editor, workshop leader and mentor.

Sally Smith enjoys creating spaces that enable encounter with God through leading Quiet Days and creating prayer corners and stations. She has led prayer groups in her local church, works as a spiritual director and writes and produces education materials.

Dorinda Miller has been leading Quiet Days and retreats in the UK and overseas, across denominations, for many years. She is currently involved in running Staying in the Vine, a six-week course on prayer and spiritual disciplines, in Nottingham.

Tony Horsfall is a freelance trainer and retreat leader based in Yorkshire, with his own ministry, Charis Training. He is an elder of Ackworth Community Church and has written several books for BRF, including *Working from a Place of Rest* (2010), *Rhythms of Grace* (2012), and most recently *Servant Ministry* (2013).

Andrea Skevington lives in Suffolk with her family. She writes for both adults and children, winning the Christian Book of the Year award (Speaking Volumes) for her retelling, *The Lion Classic Bible* (Lion Hudson, 2011). She also enjoys storytelling for children and running creative writing seminars for adults.

Sally Welch is a priest who lives and works in the centre of Oxford, working with families and young children in church. She is a writer and lecturer on spirituality and is particularly interested in pilgrimage and labyrinths. She has made many pilgrimages both in England and Europe.

Angela Ashwin is a writer and speaker on spirituality. She has written several books about prayer and life with God, including *Faith in the Fool: Risk and Delight in the Christian Adventure* (DLT, 2009) and *Woven Into Prayer: A Flexible Pattern of Daily Prayer* (Canterbury Press Norwich, 2010). She and her husband live in Southwell, Nottinghamshire.

Janet Fletcher is Team Vicar in the Rectorial Benefice of Bangor. She has contributed to *Guidelines* Bible reading notes (BRF) and is the author of *Pathway to God* (SPCK, 2006). She offers spiritual direction, and enjoys teaching groups in prayer, spirituality and faith, and leading Quiet Days and retreats.

Celtic inspiration

Helen Jaeger

There is a group of Christian men and women unique to the British Isles and Ireland, commonly referred to as the 'Celtic saints'. Names like Aidan, Brendan, Brigid, Ciaran, Columba, Cuthbert, David, Hild, Ita, Kevin and Patrick may or may not be familiar to you.

They are Christian luminaries from roughly the first millennium who share surprising similarities in their thinking and activity, whether an emphasis on caring for the poor and for social justice, embracing poverty and prayer or evangelising a non-Christian culture with gentleness, creativity and integrity.

'Celtic' Christianity has undergone something of a revival in recent years; contemporary Christians often find in these people inspiration, hope and challenge. Let's meet three of them in more detail—Brigid, Aidan and Columba—through the stories of their lives, spirituality and prayer, with a consideration of their legacy today.

For each of these saints there is a meditation in which you are invited to meet with the saint in your imagination and listen to them. These don't need to be historically accurate. Remember—symbols can speak powerfully to our spirituality. Feelings and thoughts are equally valuable ways of discerning what God might be saying to us, showing us what we value or what our personality is like and allowing God to lead us.

Perhaps you will be drawn to Brigid's motherly influence, with an emphasis on care for society, nurturing creativity, a purity of life and hospitality, or warm to Aidan's gentle and discerning approach to evangelism, his embrace of poverty, simple lifestyle and confident prayer life. On the other hand, Columba may attract you with his love of travelling, emphasis on spiritual community, giftedness and contemporary understanding of Christ.

Whichever saint draws you most, next time you are planning to travel, why not incorporate a deliberate spiritual element? Maybe you can go to a place that has a reputation for spirituality, such as Iona or Lindisfarne. Read up on an interesting Christian place and bring some of its flavour into your life, environment and prayer.

Brigid—righteous mother

Brigid was born in Ireland in around AD450. According to biographers, her parents were Dubthach, a pagan chieftain, and Brocca, a Christian slave, who herself was probably baptised by St Patrick. Brigid's reputation as a holy woman was prophesied even before she was born. The story goes like this: one day Brigid's father and mother were in a chariot passing by the cottage of an old man. Curious about the chariot, the old man asked who the woman was within it. Dubthach told him that it was Brocca, a slave whom he had made pregnant. The old man immediately exclaimed, 'Marvellous will be the child that is in her womb. No one on earth will be like her.'

Dubthach then explained to the old man that his wife wanted to sell this slave woman's child. 'Never mind,' came the reply, 'for the offspring of your wife will serve the offspring of your slave. This slave will bring forth a radiant daughter, who will shine like the sun among the stars of heaven.'

In fact, Dubthach gave his baby daughter the name of a goddess from his own religion—Brigid, the goddess of fire. But the old man's prophecy came true and Brigid's life shone, like fire, to enlighten and warm many.

As a child, Brigid proved to be pious. She gave a jewel-encrusted sword of her father's to a poor man. Her one wish was to become a nun. Eventually her father, bemused by her continual generosity towards the poor, agreed to her desire. She took the veil, committing her life solely to God.

Brigid always considered the poor, the ill and the old. A man suffering from leprosy came to Brigid to ask for a cow. Brigid asked the sick man what seemed better to him: to have a cow or to be healed. The man replied that he preferred to be healed, whereupon Brigid prayed and he was indeed completely healed.

We might call Brigid's life one of Christian social activism—caring for women, the poor, the ill and the weak in particular, and excluding no one.

Reflection point: the complexity of Brigid's social status—her father as chief and her mother as slave—perhaps influenced her concern for social justice. As you look at your life, can you see the contours of your own journey of faith? Where might God be leading you now?

Brigid's spirituality

Brigid's profession as a nun was unique. It is said that Bishop Mel, presiding over the ceremony, apparently read the form of ordaining a bishop over Brigid. MacCaille, Bishop Mel's assistant, complained that a bishop's rank had been given to a woman in the church. Bishop Mel replied, 'But I do not have any power in this matter. That dignity has been given by God to Brigid.'

Far from entering into a secluded spirituality, Brigid became an active, energetic and profound influencer of society. Not long after her profession, she formed a double monastery for monks and nuns at Kildare. The Abbey of Kildare became one of the most influential cultural, artistic and spiritual centres in the whole of Ireland and was famous throughout Christian Europe. The centre influenced thousands of people. Women, in particular, came to it to acquire skills, education and a direction for life.

Kildare was a hotspot for academics, creative people and spiritual seekers. The art school at Kildare produced the now lost *Book of*

Kildare, an illustrated book of the Gospels, which was described by one contemporary as 'the work of angels and not human skill'. It was reputedly even more lavish than the famous *Book of Kells*.

So, let's meet Brigid. Imagine you have been working for a long time in the fields near your home. You've heard about a centre that a woman called Brigid has set up. The desire to travel to visit this spiritual place has grown in you. One day, you tell your friends and family that you are going away and put together some provisions for your journey. As you travel, you ask for God's blessing and a fresh revelation of his love for you.

After a few days, you reach Brigid's centre. As you approach this place, what do you see? What do you hear? What impression does it make on your senses?

You are welcomed warmly into this centre. A member of the community comes towards you, smiling. She asks if you are staying for a few days. You reply, yes, you are. What else does she say to you? As you stand in the hallway, what catches your attention?

Next, she shows you to your room. How is it furnished? Soon after settling in, you are invited for a meal. What do you eat? Who else is there?

You spend the next few days in this centre, taking part in various activities. You also meet Brigid. What do you talk about? What issues on your heart do you share with her, and what does she say to you? Finally, the day comes for you to leave. You ask for a blessing from Brigid. Listen carefully to what she says to you.

Brigid and prayer

Brigid is recognised not only in Western spirituality, but also in the East. In Orthodox spirituality, there are several hymns to Brigid of Kildare. Here are just two examples:

O holy Brigid, you became sublime through your humility,
And flew on the wings of your longing for God.
When you arrived in the eternal City
And appeared before your Divine Spouse,
Wearing the crown of virginity,
You kept your promise
To remember those who have recourse to you.
You shower grace upon the world
And multiply miracles.
Intercede with Christ our God
That He may save our souls.

At the Church of the Oak,
Thou didst establish thy sacred monasteries
For those that took up the Tree of life,
Even the Precious Cross, upon their shoulders.
And by thy grace-filled life and love of learning,
Thou didst bear fruit a hundredfold
And didst thereby nourish the faithful.
O righteous Mother Brigid,
Intercede with Christ, the True Vine, that He save our souls.

Reflection point: are there particular symbols or phrases in the songs above that attract you? Take a phrase and play with it. Could you use it to compose your own song, prayer or other response to God?

Brigid's legacy

An emphasis on creativity and hospitality is a recognised hallmark of Celtic spirituality—a worldview that prized storytelling, poetry, music, craftsmanship, charity, justice and generosity.

One story concerns Brigid on a journey, seeking hospitality for herself and her companions at a king's court. The king, his harpers and bard were absent. However, the princes at court did the best they could to offer a warm welcome. After a short meal, Brigid, noticing some harps hanging on the wall, asked those present to offer music to the gathered guests. Regretfully, the princes declined. 'Alas, we are unable,' they said. 'However, if you bless our hands, we will do all we can to fulfil your wish.' Brigid touched their hands and prayed. The young men played so beautifully that it held the audience captivated. The gift was not given for that night only—the princes retained the skill of making beautiful music for the rest of their lives.

Reflection point: practise generous and creative hospitality. Who could you invite for a meal or coffee? We may never know at first what might be the consequences of such kindness. Could you ask for or be open to a blessing from your guests?

Aidan of Lindisfarne—man of simplicity

Irish by birth, Aidan travelled to Northumbria at the request of King Oswald to convert his English subjects. Aidan's brother monks had chosen him for the job because they knew he would be gentle and kind.

At first, a more rigid man had been sent, who had preached unsuccessfully to the English. This man had returned to his community to report that the people he'd tried to convert were 'intractable, stubborn and barbaric'. After some discussion, Aidan had said, 'It seems to me, brother, that you have been unreasonably harsh concerning your hearers. You did not first offer them the milk of simpler teaching, as the apostle recommends, so that gradually, as they grew strong on the food of God's word, they were capable of receiving more elaborate instruction and of carrying out the higher commandment of God.'

In view of Aidan's comment, the community had sent him to instruct the king's subjects instead. On his arrival, King Oswald granted Aidan the island of Lindisfarne for his home—an island that is cut off twice a day by the tide. The king, who had been an exile in Ireland, acted as Aidan's interpreter.

Aidan taught many things, not just in his words, but by his lifestyle, too. He was a strong advocate of practising what he preached. This added to the integrity of his witness. Aidan lived and taught among the English for the rest of his life, dying 17 years after his arrival in England.

Reflection point: 'to evangelise' means 'to pass on the good news'. In what ways did Aidan seek to do this? Apart from direct preaching, how might our attitude to others reflect our gospel values more closely?

Aidan's spirituality

Aidan strongly advocated a simple lifestyle. His passionate love of goodness was tempered by his gentleness and moderation, but he was not afraid to rebuke rich people, if he thought it necessary. Despite this (or perhaps because of the way in which he did it), he often received lavish gifts, many of which he passed on to people poorer than himself.

Aidan had a habit of walking everywhere, mainly so that he could fall into conversation with whomever he met, either to strengthen them in the faith or to offer them the good news. King Oswain, who supported Aidan after Oswald's death, was concerned that Aidan had to walk everywhere, and gave him a horse—perhaps similar to a rich person giving someone a car now. Aidan accepted the gift but promptly gave it to a beggar who asked for alms. When the king questioned him later, Aidan asked if he considered the beggar of less value than Aidan himself—calling into question the king's attitudes to equality and dignity.

The king, aware that Aidan had discerned his thoughts, at once threw himself at Aidan's feet and begged for forgiveness. Aidan was impressed by this man's humility and prophesied that so humble a king was worthy of eternal life.

Reflection point: how could you live more simply? Are there ways that you could live more fully with less? What might this look like in your own life and how might this make you more open to others?

Aidan and prayer

Although Aidan led an active life and encouraged his admirers to do the same, prayer was also a pivotal part of his life. He often went to

Lindisfarne to pray and be in solitude—something that must have been helped by the tidal nature of the island.

At one time, an army under Penda was attacking Northumbria. On a cruel crusade throughout the region, Penda had reached the city of Bamburgh. Unable to capture it by siege or assault, he planned to set fire to it. Penda took flammable materials—house beams, wood, wattle, rafters, thatch—from neighbouring settlements by force, laid them around the city and set them alight. Aidan was on the island of Farne at the time and saw the smoke and flames. Raising his eyes to heaven, he prayed with tears, 'Ah Lord, see how much evil Penda is doing!' As soon as he said these words, the wind turned from the city towards Penda's army instead. The army were so terrified that they stopped laying siege to the city.

Reflection point: are there situations in the world or in your community about which you feel strongly? Aidan interceded and, like Mary with Jesus at the tomb of Lazarus, was able to leave his concerns with the Lord, offering a heartfelt prayer of simplicity that, at face value, simply seemed to bring the situation to the Lord's attention. Does this way of prayer appeal to you? Is there perhaps a confidence about it that you find interesting or even challenging? How about practising this faith-filled and simple style of prayer for a week or so, to experience what it is like?

Aidan's legacy

Social justice is an important part of the work of many charities today, as is the call to a simpler lifestyle. Aidan was certainly a fearless advocate and icon for this. Is this something that we can embrace more purposefully in our own lives, communities and churches?

Similarly, Aidan and his brother monks were not afraid to have robust discussions and to be receptive to the requests of other people, admitting their failures, challenging each other and looking for new, creative solutions. Such a spirit of openness, collaboration, honest exploration and decision-making may appeal to you.

Imagine yourself at the threshold to your home. You hear a knock at the door. You open it to see Jesus standing there. He is smiling and wants to visit you. You welcome him in and ask him to help you to live more simply, guided by his values of love and freedom. Watch what he does and says as he enters your home.

You take Jesus into your living room. What does this say about your lifestyle? What does Jesus notice and what does he say to you? Is there anything you want to say to or do for him? After spending a while together in your living room, you invite him into your kitchen. Listen and talk to him in this place, too. Be completely open.

Next, you take him to your bedroom. You invite him into this intimate space. What does he do and how does he behave? How does it make you feel, having Jesus in your house like this? What do you learn about Jesus? What do you learn about yourself?

Perhaps you take him into other areas of your home—your garden, bathroom, office, even loft. Listen and speak to him in all these places.

St Columba of Iona—dove of the church

Columba (also known as Columcille) was born in AD521 into a royal clan in Donegal, western Ireland. His birth, like that of Brigid, was surrounded by prophecy. His mother dreamed that a great cloak was given to her. This cloak reached from one part of Ireland all the way to Scotland and contained the colours of the rainbow. In her dream, a young man took the cloak from her. She was sad, but the youth said to her, 'Lady, you have no need to be sad—rather, be joyful and radiant. You will have a son. The whole of Ireland and Scotland will be full of his teaching.'

After ordination and after founding many monasteries, Columba left Ireland at the age of 42 and arrived at Iona, an island off the Scottish coast, where he formed a large spiritual community. He had taken with him 20 bishops, 40 priests, 30 deacons and 50 students! They reached Iona on the night of Pentecost and Columba said, 'It is well that we plant our roots here on this soil.'

Columba was a gifted poet, academic and writer. As well as travelling, he loved solitude, learning and natural beauty. Columba means 'dove of the church'.

Columba died and was buried at Iona. Even his death pointed to his deep spirituality—as he died he had a vision of angels and his face was marked with a shining joy.

Reflection point: one old retreat practice was to ask participants to meditate on their death, as a way of getting in touch with how to live well. If you were going to write a (non-morbid!) obituary of your own life, what elements would you want to include? What does this say about your life now? What would you like to change in the obituary? How could you do this?

Columba's spirituality

Columba had a strong sense of place and blessed everywhere he visited. He said of one favourite place:

> *For this do I love Derry,*
> *For its smoothness, for its purity,*
> *Because it is full of white angels*
> *From one end to the other.*

He also begged three gifts from God: chastity, wisdom and pilgrimage. He was granted all three.

Reflection point: Columba valued wisdom. Consider this: 'My goal is that they may… know the mystery of God, namely, Christ, in whom are hidden all the treasures of wisdom and knowledge' (Colossians 2:2–4, NIV). Why not take a walk in your favourite place and reflect on the riches and wisdom that you experience, thanking God for them?

Alternatively, if you were going to ask God for three gifts, like Columba, what would they be?

Columba and prayer

It is said that in every place in which Columba set up a spiritual community there were groves of oak trees (considered a pagan or druid tree). Coming into contact with pagan culture was a feature of Celtic spirituality; the awareness of forces at work other than Christian ones was common to the lives of many Celtic saints.

One account claims that Columba addressed Jesus as 'my druid'. This does not mean that he accepted pagan belief, but that he gently taught his followers a better way. His exact words were, 'There is no "streod" that can tell our fate nor bird upon the bough, nor trunk of gnarled oak. I adore not the voices of birds nor chance, nor the love of son or wife—my Druid is Christ, the Son of God.'

Columba was able to use the language and culture of his hearers to point them to Christian belief and prayer. Rather than destroying culture or place, in his wisdom Columba aimed to return what was good to its creator, his beloved Christ.

Reflection point: Columba used the term 'my druid' to express his personal relationship of humility and spirituality towards Christ. What term might be meaningful for you (Christ my leader, my helper, my star, for example)?

Columba's legacy

Even today, Iona is a well-known place of pilgrimage and spirituality. People who visit Iona describe it as a 'thin place, where heaven and earth meet'—in itself a Celtic idea. You can find out more by going to www.iona.org.uk.

In the continuing spirit of Celtic Christianity, there is an emphasis on learning, prayer, worship, creativity, exploration, hospitality, retreat and social justice. Many people take the time to travel to Iona, to stay in a place of spiritual community, to pray, to rest and to be refreshed for their work. This is exactly what Columba's life was about, and his legacy lives on very clearly.

Imagine that you are part of the community that Columba has brought with him to Iona from Ireland. It's the first night of your arrival. You are lying in bed, remembering the journey to England. What are the sights, smells and thoughts that fill your mind?

In the morning you wake and take part in community chores—perhaps making breakfast, establishing comfortable dwelling places, exploring the island or finding provisions. How does it feel to know that this is your new home?

After a few days, Columba gathers the community together. He asks you all how you are feeling about your new environment and invites each member of the community to speak. When your turn comes, what do you say and what concerns do you raise?

Weeks pass and you are feeling more settled in your new home. One day, while you are working, Columba approaches you and asks to have a word. He thanks you for your input to the community and asks if you feel that your concerns are being met. You answer him and note his response. Columba then gives you a particular job to do. What is it?

A feast of thanksgiving

Sally Smith

Sukkot and harvest

Sukkot is the Jewish festival in which the harvest of fruit is celebrated. Earlier in the year the harvest of grain has already been celebrated, and now with the fruit gathering, harvest is completed. This year Sukkot will be marked for the eight days from 18 to 25 September.

During the celebration of Sukkot, families build a tabernacle (*sukkah*), in which they should, ideally, live for the eight days of the festival. In reality, many eat meals in their *sukkah*, but not all sleep there.

At a time when they are feeling most secure, God calls his children to live in temporary shelters, reminding them of their continuing dependence on him, and the dependence of their ancestors as they escaped from Egypt and spent 40 years in the desert.

The overriding emotion of the festival is rejoicing. God's people are called to rejoice, to remember God's provision; and with the festival coming a few days after Yom Kippur (the feast of atonement when all sins are forgiven) there is additional reason for rejoicing as they 'start again' with God.

Sukkot is a time of thanksgiving, when thanks for food are joined with thanks for God's generous provision to his people in other ways. So, we remember Abraham looking to the stars to see how many will be his descendents. It is a reminder of the 40 years spent in the wilderness and of God's presence with the people of Israel during that period as he sheltered them with his presence (in a pillar of cloud by day and a pillar of fire by night), fed them with manna, provided water and gave them his law.

It joins the ideas of God being our shelter with God sheltering with us, and rejoicing in his generous provision for us.

There are several traditions and rituals around this festival, and we will consider these and their implications for Christians. Jesus, as a Jew, celebrated Sukkot, as recorded in John's Gospel (see John 7), and we shall look at the events around his celebration in the temple.

With the act of moving into the *sukkah*, Sukkot becomes a time of stripping away and being reliant on God. This might be a good time to consider where you pray and how much you rely on the trappings around that space. Is your focus being taken away from God and your dependence on him? Maybe somewhere less comfortable would help you rejoice in God's provision for you. Or it might be that you don't have a specific place for prayer, and this could be a good time to create one. It doesn't have to be a separate building, like a *sukkah*; it could be a corner of a room, marked in some way as a place where encounter with God is expected.

As with Christian harvest celebrations, Sukkot is a time for remembering God's generosity to us, rejoicing in what we have, and recognising where it came from and how we can share it with others.

So may you rejoice this Sukkot.

Fruit thanksgiving

Sukkot is the time when the fruit harvest is celebrated. Let's spend some time recognising and being thankful for fruit.

Take an apple. You can use another fruit if you prefer—just adapt the words that follow to suit what you have chosen.

Pause and acknowledge that you have an apple in your hand.

Recognise it as part of God's creation.

Look at it carefully. See its colours and patterns. Feel the rough and smooth of the skin. Wonder at its creation, at what happened in its growth to make it what it is now. Notice the blemishes and bruises, the asymmetry of its shape. It is often the imperfections that make fruit interesting and the less perfect have the better taste. Enjoy the apparent faults and what they add to the look of the apple.

Smell it.

Notice the stalk, which has carried the nutrients to the fruit over the months it has been growing on the tree.

What has happened to this fruit between the tree and your hand? Allow the apple to tell you its story. Listen and hear what it has been through to make it the apple it is.

Be aware of God holding you, just as you hold the apple; of his looking at you, just as you looked at the apple; of his listening to your story and hearing how you became the person you are today. Allow him to love you and appreciate your blemishes as well as your beauty, to see the potential in you.

Then, when you're ready, cut or bite into the apple.

Taste. Enjoy the juices. Hear the crunch. Feel it as you chew. Enjoy each mouthful as you eat it slowly. What are you thinking? What is this apple like inside? What from its past has made it so good to eat?

It was grown to be eaten. As you eat, allow the juice to come out.

Find a pip. Look at it. See the beauty, the potential in this tiny thing.

Ask God that you may be used as he intended, that the sweetness he has given you may be shared with others.

Enjoy finishing the apple and thank God for his generous provision.

Feed the hungry

Jewish people living in a *sukkah* for a week have the opportunity to remember good times and bad. They remember the times when their ancestors had plenty and the times when they had little or no food and relied on God daily.

Most of us can't imagine what it would be like to rely utterly on God for food. We have full cupboards and freezers and well-stocked local shops for the 'essentials' we may have forgotten in the big weekly shop. Most of us have never known what it is like to be able to provide only one small meal a day for our families, and not to know where next week's meals are coming from, or even where tomorrow's meal is coming from.

God promised Moses a land 'flowing with milk and honey' (Exodus 3:8, NRSV), a term we still use to describe abundance and plenty. In the wilderness God provided manna for his people (see Exodus 16). They were instructed to take as much as they needed for each day; not more than enough 'just in case', as it wouldn't keep, but enough for their families for that day.

Jesus later taught his disciples not to worry about what they were going to eat (Matthew 6:25), but also to be active in making sure that the hungry were fed and the thirsty given something to drink (25:35).

As you eat your meals today, recognise God's provision for you and your family. What riches has he given you in your food and choices? Eat with greater enjoyment and appreciation of his generosity.

You could consider what you do towards making sure the hungry are fed, locally or globally.

Under the sun

The festival of Sukkot comes as the whole of the harvest is gathered in. The barns are full and there is a sense of provision for the year ahead. There is plenty of food, and everyone could expect to relax and take it easy for a while. But with the taking it easy and the plentifulness comes complacency. It is easy in the times of plenty not to remember the harder times. It is easy to forget how to rely on God when we don't need to rely on him for our basic needs.

So, it is at this time of plenty that God called his people to leave their comfort and remember the hard times of their ancestors by moving out into temporary, insecure accommodation. It is not surprising that this is a time when the book of Ecclesiastes is read.

Ecclesiastes reminds us that humans are made from the earth; and in that sense we are like the harvest that has just been collected, which grew from the earth. It also describes an emptiness of existence that is irrespective of the amount of wealth or riches owned. It causes us to ponder, whether this is all there is under the sun. That is the significance: under the sun. Under the sun, growing and dying is all there is. But if we get beyond the sun, away from earth-bound thoughts, and reach out to God (seen by the first readers of Ecclesiastes as being beyond the sun), we begin to have a spiritual existence, which adds meaning. The ordinary life going on under the sun is transformed into a holy act. As the sun shines though the flimsy roof of the *sukkah*, so we, although rooted in the earth, can be reaching beyond the sun to nurture that special spark which leads to a life with meaning and hope and substance.

Solomon discovers that all his riches do not bring him happiness; and the time spent in the *sukkah* emphasises living in the moment, spending time with family and friends, and acts as a reminder that it is these simple things that bring pleasure. Everything is temporary, and so Solomon advises enjoying everything in its proper season: not trying to save happiness for tomorrow, but embracing it today.

Slowly read Ecclesiastes 1:2–11, asking God to show you how different life is with him there to give it meaning and purpose. Be reminded of the blessing God gives and the colour he adds to your life.

Manna in the desert

Sukkot is a time of remembering God's provision to his people in the wilderness, his feeding them with manna and quails (Exodus 16). Imagine joining the Israelites as they wander in the desert.

Look at the thousands of people there, hungry and thirsty. Feel the heat and the dryness of the desert.

Listen to the complaining that is happening around you. Listen as someone tells of the bitter water they drank and another complains of how hungry they feel. It is several weeks since they left Egypt, which is beginning to seem preferable to this place. They remember the problems, but they also remember the food and the drink, which wasn't plentiful, but was better than what they're getting now.

You become aware of a quietness among the people and see Moses and Aaron standing ready to talk to them. Aaron says, 'God has heard your complaining. He is going to give you bread in the morning and meat in the evening. You will know that he is God because he will give you bread in the morning and meat in the evening.'

How does this make you feel? What are the people around you saying? Are they grateful or sceptical? Do they believe God can do this?

Aaron continues, 'You can take as much bread and meat as you need. But don't take too much—just what you and your family need. If you take too much, it will go mouldy overnight.'

The cloud of the glory of God comes close to Moses and Aaron. Moses looks at you and calls you to join him. Walk through the crowd towards Moses. Then walk with Moses towards the cloud. You are to meet with God. What do you say to God about what you have just seen and heard? How does God respond? Do you have a conversation about his provision for you?

Listen and talk to God until it is time to leave.

Spend a few moments praying through what God has said and his provision for you.

The roof of the sukkah

The roof of a *sukkah* (tabernacle) should be made of materials that grow from the ground (branches and leaves), representing the clouds of glory that guided and protected the Israelites in the desert after leaving Egypt. The roof should have enough of a covering so that there is more shade than sun during the day, but the stars can still be seen at night.

The stars are a reminder of God's covenant with Abram and God's promise that Abram's descendants would be as numerous as the stars in the sky.

Go outside and spend some time with Abram looking at the stars. It might be best to take a blanket to lie on to protect your neck. With Abram, hear God saying, 'Look toward heaven and count the stars, if you are able to count them' (Genesis 15:5). Imagine what it might have felt like for an old man with no children to be told that his descendants would outnumber the stars. Try counting them. Remember that in most of this country we see only a small number of the stars and that there are many, many more of them we can't see.

God went on to remind Abram of his calling.

Spend some time with God, looking at the stars. What does he want to tell you through them? What are his uncountable gifts to you? What has he called you to already? What might still be to come? What seems impossible at the moment? Offer these to the God who made the heavens and who can give an old man descendants that equal the stars.

Tabernacle

As well as for the shelters used at Sukkot, the word 'tabernacle' is also used in the Old Testament for the dwelling place of God. The Israelites were ordered to build a tabernacle, a place where God would dwell in their midst. As they travelled through the desert and into new lands, they took the tabernacle with them; God dwelt in the midst of their community and was present with them.

As Christians we are familiar with Christ coming to live with his people—Immanuel, God with us, living with us and dwelling at a specific time and place among us. John uses this idea when he says, 'And the word became flesh and lived among us' (John 1:14), literally meaning 'God pitched his tent among us'. In that dwelling was the fullness of God's glory and his grace and truth. Similarly, in the wilderness God's glory filled the tabernacle and it was shrouded in the cloud of glory.

In the Psalms we read of God providing shelter from troubles around and inviting us to shelter with him as a place of refuge.

Look up Psalm 27. As you read the psalm, draw what you are reading. Don't worry about artistic merit, but use symbols, lines and marks that represent the psalm to you. They don't need to be understood or seen by anyone else. Create the shelter of the house of the Lord and indicate the enemies outside. See where God has put you high on a rock and draw the level path. What do these represent? Allow God to show you his glory and his refuge as you draw. Offer sacrifices of songs to God and rest in his house. Receive in this place the confidence that comes from being in his presence and surrounded by his strength and light. You could keep your drawing as a reminder of God as the stronghold of your life.

The four species

'On the first day you shall take the fruit of majestic trees, branches of palm trees, boughs of leafy trees, and willows of the brook; and you shall rejoice before the Lord your God for seven days.'
LEVITICUS 23:40

Leviticus specifies that the branches of three trees are to be brought together with the fruit of a fourth tree and to be included in the rejoicing.

The branches used are the lulav (a type of date palm), myrtle and willow. A branch of each is tied together and shaken in six directions (in front, behind, to each side, above and below) and then brought together with the etrog fruit—similar to a lemon but sweeter.

There are different interpretations for the meaning behind these actions. Sometimes each represents a different part of the body:

- The lulav, which is always the longest, represents the backbone;
- Myrtle for the eyes;
- Willow for the lips;
- Etrog for the heart.

These can then be related to prayer.

The etrog is initially held upside down, then turned the right way up when it meets with God. We are 'upside down' until we meet with God.

The eyes are turned down towards reality, representing what we are praying for.

The lips are the consciousness of who is praying and ask the question: is it God praying or the person?

The backbone represents standing in the silent devoted upright state.

Or, if taste represents learning and smell represents good deeds, then these four species between them stand for all kinds of people in these two respects. The etrog has both taste and smell, the lulav has taste but no smell, myrtle has smell but no taste, and willow has neither taste nor smell, so their joining together represents creating a community of the different types of people, woven together to become one. This is emphasised as the four species are shaken in each direction, bringing people from all corners of the earth together before God.

Think about a community you are part of, or know well. Who are the people with taste, who are those with smell, and who have both or neither? Taste and smell could be the traditional learning and deeds or other pairs of attributes. Recognise how each individual brings their strengths to the community and how those are woven into the identity of the community. Are there times when you have failed to appreciate what someone is bringing or have bemoaned what they don't bring? Or times when you have not brought all you could, and the community has been the poorer for it?

The etrog also represents the stranger. How is the stranger welcomed in this community? Spend some time holding individuals and the community before God and praising him for the variety.

Prayers and blessings

O give thanks to the Lord, for he is good, for his steadfast love endures forever.
PSALM 136:1

Below are adaptations of traditional Sukkot blessings. As you read them and use them, consider which draws you and expresses what you would like to ask of God. How would you want to rephrase any of them to make them relevant to you today?

Take one of the blessings below, or one that you have devised yourself, and repeat it throughout the day, thereby asking God's blessing on parts of your life you might previously have been taking for granted. Alternatively, create a habit of adapting these blessings frequently during the day, asking God's blessing on aspects of what you are doing or where you are.

Blessed are you, Lord our God, king of the universe, who sanctifies us with his commandments and commands us to light the candles of the holiday.

Blessed are you, Lord our God, master of the universe, who has granted us life and sustained us and who has enabled us to reach this time.

Blessed are you, Lord our God, king of the universe, who has given us holidays, customs and seasons of happiness.

Blessed are you, Lord our God, master of the universe, who sanctifies us with his commandments and commanded us to dwell in the sukkah.

Blessed are you, Lord our God, king of the universe, who has sanctified us with his commandments and has commanded us concerning the waving of the lulav.

Light

As well as water, light is significant at Sukkot. In biblical times, each evening the temple would be flooded with light. There would be huge braziers lighting the way, and in the Court of the Women, where most people would gather, there would be hundreds of candles lit.

The light would shine across Jerusalem, lighting up every courtyard, and from a distance the city would be clearly seen, glistening like a jewel. Into this ceremony of light John places Jesus and his statement, 'I am the light of the world' (John 8:12). What a different impact these words must have had for being spoken in a feast of light!

Jesus was building not only on the visual image for the festival, but on Old Testament images of the servant of the Lord as a light to the nations (Isaiah 42:6). In the wilderness the Israelites followed a cloud by day and a pillar of fire by night, and it was this pillar of fire that was being remembered in the temple at this time. The Lord and the salvation he brings are related to light ('The Lord is my light and my salvation', Psalm 27:1). In Matthew 5:14 Jesus calls his disciples to be a light for the world. He now takes the step of claiming to be the light of the world that will remove the darkness from life and give meaning and purpose.

He promises that whoever follows him will have light all their life and will never walk in the dark again, and he says it at a time when he is surrounded by light in the midst of the festival.

Take a torch or lamp and light up some dark places in your home or garden. Notice how powerfully the light takes over the darkness. Notice the contrast between light and dark. See how far the light travels. Create a bright light and read John 8:12 and John 1:6–9.

Water from the pool of Siloam

Every day during the feast of Tabernacles, water from the pool of Siloam is poured into silver bowls on the altar and allowed to flow over the altar as an offering to God. In the heat of the country and at the end of the summer this would be an extravagant and costly act when water was becoming scarce. It was also a prophetic act, anticipating the promise of water in Ezekiel 47, and a sign of trust that God would send rain in the coming months.

In John 7 we have a record of Jesus celebrating the feast of Tabernacles, and it is on the last day of that festival that he cries out, 'Let anyone who is thirsty come to me, and let the one who believes in me drink. As the scripture has said, "Out of the believer's heart shall flow rivers of living water"' (John 7:37–38). Two things are happening in this passage. Jesus is inviting his listeners to drink of the living water he brings—to receive the Holy Spirit and the gifts that he can give. He is also calling them to allow those rivers to flow out of them. He is calling them to allow the Holy Spirit to work in them and then to use them to work for others. For his listeners this was still at some point in the future. They were expecting the outpouring of the Holy Spirit at the dawning of the new age.

Ezekiel 47 describes the new Jerusalem and the new temple, and how rivers would flow from them and produce fresh water and vegetation. Jesus suggests that this will be fulfilled in individuals; that the waters of the spirit will flow from people's hearts, rather than from the temple.

Read the following passages from the Old Testament that refer to God pouring out his spirit as water:

- Isaiah 12:3
- Isaiah 44:3
- Isaiah 55:1
- Isaiah 58:11
- Zechariah 14:8

Spend some time with these, allowing God to paint the pictures they describe in your imagination, and receiving the Holy Spirit afresh as living water. Allow the Holy Spirit to water all that you do, as the rain waters the land.

Rejoice

Rejoice during your festival... for the Lord your God will bless you in all your produce and in all your undertakings, and you shall surely celebrate.
DEUTERONOMY 16:14–15

Sukkot is a festival of rejoicing. The whole harvest has been gathered in, and it completes the celebrations of harvest after an earlier celebration of the gathering of the grain harvest.

As well as celebrating the gathering of the harvest, Sukkot is a time of remembering all God's provision for his people over time, including his provision in the wilderness and his acts of salvation. It comes a few days after Yom Kippur, the festival when sins are forgiven, and so there is the added rejoicing of being clean before God and in a place suitable for rejoicing.

Psalm 67 is sometimes associated with Sukkot as a call to praise God. Read it slowly until a phrase or verse calls to you. Then pause on that phrase and repeat it in your head. Allow it to enter your brain and then to go deeper into you, to become part of you. Allow God to speak to you through the phrase, and use it to connect with him.

The earth has yielded its increase;
God, our God has blessed us.
PSALM 67:6

The Lord's Prayer

Dorinda Miller

Opening up to the prayer

Jesus' prayer in Matthew 6:9–13, known as the Lord's Prayer, must be the most well-known and oft-repeated prayer in the Bible. It is the model that Jesus gave to his disciples in response to their request that he teach them to pray, and is widely and regularly used across denominations.

As a child I was brought up to recite it aloud before I went to sleep each night—to the extent that when I was very small I believed that one couldn't actually go to sleep unless it had been said!

However, I found that overfamiliarity through frequent use at home, school and church lessened its importance and impact for me—although at times of crisis, even when my faith was low and dim, I found I defaulted to it. As my faith grew and strengthened, so the prayer's power and relevance became more important, and in recent years I have had some memorable experiences of using it, especially on prayer trips in the Middle East.

So, whatever your experience and views of this prayer are, I would like to invite you to journey through the next fortnight with anticipation and expectation that God will reveal more of himself to you as you ponder anew on the Lord's Prayer.

The Lord's Prayer begins with praise, moves to priorities, and considers provision, personal relationships and protection, before ending where it started, with praise.

Try reading the Lord's Prayer in three different versions, if you have access to them.

Read each one slowly three times and ask the Lord to highlight to you the verses he wants to use to speak to you.

In the silence, listen to what he says to you.

Record the insights in your journal.

Spend time praising him for who he is and for all that he has been to you in the past; for all that he is to you now in the present; and for all that he will be to you in the future.

Walk of thanksgiving and praise

Our father which art in heaven, hallowed be thy name.
MATTHEW 6:9 (KJV)

The Lord's Prayer begins with the recognition that God is our father in heaven and that he is holy. We respond to his holiness by giving him glory, worship and praise. There are many ways to do this. However, I would like to suggest that you do this today by going for a walk of praise and thanksgiving, using the framework that Jesus gave his disciples in Acts 1:8, where he told them that they would be his witnesses 'in Jerusalem, in all Judea and Samaria, and to the ends of the earth' (NIV). Often being outside and being on the move can bring a different dimension to prayer and your surroundings, and creation can inspire you, speak to you and encourage you.

Begin your walk by being thankful for what you have, where you are.

Then continue with thanksgiving for the wider community, before moving on to focus on thanksgiving for the country in which you live and the wider world.

Complete your walk with a time of praise, either aloud or in silence, using songs, psalms, and hymns.

It may be that your circumstances preclude an actual walk, in which case you might like to sit quietly and spend time in thanksgiving and praise, or do the walk using your imagination.

A final thought: In his book *Consumer Detox*, Mark Powley suggests 'spending a week where the only thing you ever do in prayer is say "thank you". That's nothing but thanksgiving for a full seven-day stretch' (Zondervan, 2011, p. 232). He found it so helpful that he has continued to do this one day a week. A few years ago, during Lent, I set myself the challenge of going for a walk of praise and thanksgiving every day before work. Like Mark, I too found it an amazing experience, and by Easter specific issues and attitudes in my life had changed significantly. I encourage you to try this exercise for yourself, and to see how God meets you through it.

Creative activity

> *Thy kingdom come, thy will be done in earth, as it is in heaven.*
> MATTHEW 6:10   .

Imagine your life as a plot of land—perhaps a garden or a field.

Draw a sketch of your land on a sheet of paper, and then the people in your life (family, friends, colleagues, neighbours).

Now add to your land the activities in which you are currently involved.

Which parts of your land are growing well?

Which parts of your land are struggling to grow?

Are there any barren areas or areas that are burnt out?

Is there any water on your land?

Which parts of your land need refreshing and irrigating?

Which parts need the wind of the Spirit to blow over them?

What type of season is your land currently going through?

Your land is part of God's kingdom. Lay it before him and review it with him.

Seek God's will for you in this season of your life. Ask him if there is anything that he wants you to put down or to pick up, so that his kingdom may grow and extend through you.

Thank God that your land is under his ownership and in his control, and pray for his blessing over it.

Matthew 13:1–58

Thy kingdom come, thy will be done in earth, as it is in heaven.
MATTHEW 6:10

If you were to look up the word 'kingdom' in a dictionary, you would see it defined as a monarchical state such as the United Kingdom or the Hashemite Kingdom of Jordan, or a territory that is subject to a king/queen, or the spiritual reign of God. If you were to look up the word in a Bible concordance, you would find approximately 155 references listed in the New Testament, approximately 107 of which were mentioned by Jesus himself.

The kingdom of God is a key theme in the Gospels, and Jesus highlights its importance, not only in his teaching, but also by including it in this prayer. The kingdom of God is not geographical, temporal or spatial. It is a gift we receive and enter into. It is not imposed upon us. We are encouraged to release and relinquish our rule/control/will and ask the Father to give us his. When we seek his kingdom and surrender our ways and wills to him, we can then become co-heirs with Christ. Where his rule is accepted, his kingdom comes.

Take a few minutes to let go of the things that are on your mind—cares, concerns, and anxious thoughts. Then pray for a spirit of wisdom and revelation as you read Matthew 13.

In this chapter Jesus likens the kingdom of heaven to:

* a man who sowed good seed in his field (v. 24)
* a mustard seed (v. 31)

- yeast (v. 33)
- treasure hidden in a field (v. 44)
- a merchant looking for pearls (v. 45)
- a net (v. 47)

Choose one of the parables (or more, if time permits) and ponder on what it means for you today.

What does the kingdom of heaven mean to you? How has your understanding of the kingdom of heaven changed over the course of your journey of faith?

How do you respond to the notion of God ruling over your life?

Pray for opportunities to share the good news of the kingdom of God in the coming week. Pray that you will recognise them when they arise and that God will give you his words to say in them.

Reflection on God's provision

Give us this day our daily bread.
MATTHEW 6:11

Traditionally, this request is viewed as asking for everything we need to keep us alive. These needs include not only food and clothing, but also spiritual needs and whatever else we may require during the course of the day. This provision is not earned; rather, it is given to us by God, who loves us. This request is also seen in the Old Testament; in Proverbs we read, 'give me only my daily bread' (Proverbs 30:8). There is also the implication that if we need daily sustenance, we need to pray daily too.

Think of all the things that God has provided for you… from your faith in him and your relationship with him, to your family, friends, home, possessions, job.

Take time to think of all these things and be thankful.

Now ponder on all the ways in recent weeks that God has provided for you, physically, spiritually, emotionally, materially, and be thankful.

If there are any ways in which you feel unprovided for, lay these before him now.

Pour out your heart to him, and then leave these concerns with him. In the stillness, listen for his response.

Record his words in your journal and thank him for what he has shown you.

Jehovah Jireh

Give us this day our daily bread.
MATTHEW 6:11

In this climate of uncertainty, financial instability, and unrest in many parts of the world, it is good to remind ourselves that God is Jehovah Jireh. This name literally means 'the Lord who sees', or 'the Lord will see to it' (see Genesis 22:12–14) and is generally taken to mean 'the Lord who provides'. He is our provider, and he will supply all that we need.

Read John 21:1–12, and then enter into the meditation below and see how Jesus provided for his disciples.

Imagine that you are with the disciples, or even that you are one of them, when Peter announces he is going fishing. Take in the surroundings as you walk to the shore. Is the moon shining? Is it cold? Imagine getting into the boat. Where do you sit? What are the disciples talking about?

How do they feel about catching no fish? You watch the sun rise. You see a man on the shore and he calls out, 'Friends, have you caught any fish?' 'No,' you all answer. He calls out again, 'Throw your net on the right side of the boat and you will find some.' How do the disciples respond to this instruction? Do they do it instantly, or comment that it will not work: there are no fish, and they have been there all night?

The net goes over the side of the boat. How do the disciples respond to the fact that there are now so many fish that they cannot haul the net in? How do you feel?

John turns to Peter and says, 'It is the Lord.' At this, Peter wraps his garment around him and jumps into the water. What is the mood of the disciples now? You reach the shore and see a fire burning with some fish on it and some bread. How do you feel? Peter gets back into the boat. The net is dragged to the shore, but it does not break.

Jesus says, 'Come and have breakfast.' He takes some bread and gives some to each of you. How do you feel as he gives you the bread, and then the fish?

He comes and stands beside you.

What do you want to say to him?

What does he say to you?

Spend time with him and, when you are ready, take your leave.

Finally, take a few minutes to praise and thank God for what he has revealed to you through entering into this meditation.

Contemplation on forgiveness

And forgive us our debts, as we forgive our debtors.
MATTHEW 6:12

Read Luke 7:36–50 a few times to familiarise yourself with the story before entering into the imaginative exercise below.

Imagine that you are at the dinner at Simon's house. Take time to observe the scene as fully as possible. Notice the people, the food, the atmosphere.

How many people are at the dinner?

Where are Simon and Jesus sitting?

Watch as the woman with the very expensive bottle of perfume enters the room.

Observe her weeping… her tears falling on the feet of Jesus… how she dries his feet with her hair.

See her pouring the perfume over his feet. As you see her do this, how do you feel about her actions? How do the other guests respond?

You hear Jesus speak to Simon.

You hear him speak to the woman: 'I forgive your sins. Your faith has saved you. Go in peace.'

How do you feel as you see the woman depart? What are you thinking?

Now Jesus comes over to you. How are you feeling? What do you want to say to him?

Take your time and tell him what is on your heart and in your mind.

Now hear him say to you, 'I forgive your sins. Your faith has saved you. Go in peace.'

Forgiveness in practice

And forgive us our debts, as we forgive our debtors.
MATTHEW 6:12

Over the course of our lives, we all experience being hurt by the words and actions of those around us. This part of the Lord's Prayer teaches us to ask God for forgiveness for the ways in which we have sinned and, in turn, to forgive those whose words or actions have hurt us. The assumption is that we will receive and give forgiveness. It is not optional. God freely forgives us (Psalm 103:12) and he expects us to do the same.

Understanding the nature of forgiveness and keeping short accounts with God and those around us are part of our journey of faith. If we do not incorporate this aspect of our faith into our lives, we will not fully experience the freedom that life in Christ brings. Jesus said that he came 'that they may have life, and have it to the full' (John 10:10).

While the aim of forgiveness is reconciliation, for a variety of reasons this may not always be achievable. Forgiveness is about a change of heart and mind, and as such we can deal only with ourselves. We are neither able to change nor responsible for changing the hearts and minds of those whose behaviour, in word or deed, has adversely impacted us. It is well documented that those who hang on to grudges and fail to engage with the process of forgiveness can experience physical, emotional and spiritual problems—though of course not all problems are caused by a lack of forgiveness!

Review

What is your experience of and current perspective on God's forgiveness to you?

What is your experience of and current perspective on forgiving yourself and others?

How do you react when you need to give or receive forgiveness? Is it easier to forgive or to be forgiven? Is there anything that prevents you from giving or receiving forgiveness?

Respond

What strategies can we employ to help us move through the process of forgiveness and on, if possible, to reconciliation?

Reflect on the times when people have forgiven you.

How did the way they did this impact you? What did you find helpful or unhelpful? Could you use any helpful ways yourself in forgiving others?

When forgiveness is difficult, how could you try and deal with this?

Would writing down the incident in your journal and leaving it with

God be helpful? Review the situation, and record the facts and your reaction.

Would a guided meditation on the event help you? Imagining the event, watching it unfurl in your mind and then pausing to see where Jesus was in it—asking him for his perspective and wisdom to help you to let go of the hurt and move on.

Would talking to and praying with an understanding and wise friend or church leader help you?

Remember

Psalm 103:10 and 13

Resisting temptation

And lead us not into temptation, but deliver us from evil.
MATTHEW 6:13

While God is Jehovah Jireh, our provider, Jesus is the Good Shepherd who cares for his sheep. As his sheep we can expect him to care for us, protect us and lead us to safety. We need to remember that our times are in God's hands and that he is in control. When we go through the waters and fire (Isaiah 43:1–2), he will be with us. In his letter to the Romans, Paul reminds us that 'we know that in all things God works for the good of those who love him, who have been called according to his purpose' (Romans 8:28).

During these times of temptation or testing or challenge, God is forming our characters and refining us, so that not only does our faith become deeper and stronger, but we also become more like Jesus. However, despite these positive aspects, times of trial and temptation can leave us feeling battered and bruised. This highlights our need for community, to be part of a small group of believers with whom we can share our lives; a place where we can give and receive encouragement and support and where we can develop and strengthen our faith. On our own and isolated, without support from fellow believers, we are far more at risk of succumbing to temptation and then of continuing to indulge in it. None of us is free from temptation; it comes in all shapes and sizes and from all quarters! It leads to sin that is not only detrimental to our own physical, emotional and spiritual well-being but can also, through our behaviour, have a serious effect on those close to us.

Creative writing activity

Respond word by word to the phrase: 'lead us not into temptation, but deliver us from evil'. Write your responses down on paper, in your journal, on your computer. For example: 'lead'—what does this word mean to you? What mental images come to you as you think about this word? What or who leads you?

When you have completed this activity, spend a few minutes reflecting on what temptation actually means for you. What tempts you? How and where? What strategies can you put in place for yourself to resist the temptations you are currently facing? Who can help and support you in this?

Finally, read Hebrews 4:14–16 and be encouraged.

Ephesians 6:10–17

And lead us not into temptation, but deliver us from evil.
MATTHEW 6:13

God is strong, and he wants you to be strong… Be prepared. You're up against far more than you can handle on your own. Take all the help you can get, every weapon God has issued, so that when it's all over but the shouting you'll still be on your feet. Truth, righteousness, peace, faith, and salvation are more than words. Learn how to apply them. You'll need them throughout your life. God's Word is an indispensable weapon. In the same way prayer is essential in this ongoing warfare. Pray hard and long.
EPHESIANS 6:10, 13–18 *The Message*

Traditional translations of the Bible show Paul using the imagery of a soldier wearing armour to encourage believers to stand firm and fight everything that the devil throws at them. However, Eugene Peterson in The Message emphasises that truth, righteousness, peace, faith and salvation are more than words, and we need to learn how to apply them in our fight against evil. In some ways this is reminiscent of the story of David and Goliath in 1 Samuel 17. King Saul gave David armour to put on but he found it cumbersome, preferring instead to select five smooth stones. Proclaiming that he was coming against Goliath in the name of the Lord, he selected a stone, put it in his sling and shot Goliath dead with it.

While God's word and prayer are indispensable weapons in our fight, perhaps the concept of carrying the five stones of truth, righteousness, peace, faith and salvation in a small bag with us at all times, and asking God to show us exactly which one to use and how to use it in each battle we face, will also help us to fight, to stand our ground and to overcome.

Reflect on your use of the weapons and ask God to increase your understanding and insight into their use.

Psalm 29

For thine is the kingdom, and the power and the glory for ever and ever. Amen
MATTHEW 6:13

Read Psalm 29 out aloud in more than one version.

Choose a word, phrase or verse to ponder on for five to ten minutes.

What does the Lord want to show you through your chosen verse?

Write down your insights in your journal.

Hesychasm is a tradition within the Eastern Church that refers to the practice of repeating a simple prayer over and over again. The thinking behind this is that, by repeating the prayer, we can focus our thoughts on God so that he can enter our heart.

The LORD gives strength to his people; the LORD blesses his people with peace.
PSALM 29:11

Use this verse as *hesychastic* prayer for ten minutes a day over the next few days.

Praying the Lord's Prayer through actions

Have you ever experimented with putting actions to portions of psalms or songs? It can be an enriching experience. I would like to invite you either to create your own actions or to use the following as you recite the Lord's Prayer. You may choose to recite it out loud or silently to yourself.

Stand with your feet a little way apart. As you say 'Our Father who art in heaven', lift one arm up above your head, and as you say 'hallowed be your name', lift the other arm up and bring your hands together as in prayer. Lower your arms to your side.

Repeat the action of lifting first one arm and then the other as you say, 'Thy kingdom come, thy will be done.' As you say 'on earth', make your fingers touch above your head, then open your arms out sideways and bring them down so that your fingers gently touch in front of your body. Point towards heaven with one hand as you say, 'as it is in heaven'.

Cup your hands together and stretch out your arms as you say, 'Give us this day our daily bread,' and bring them back towards your body and mime eating, by bringing your fingers towards your lips.

Cross your arms across your body so that your right hand touches your left shoulder and your left hand touches your right shoulder, and bow your head as you say, 'Forgive us our debts,' then uncross your arms and stretch your arms out with your hands together, take a step forward and move them from side to side, to symbolise forgiving those around you.

As you say, 'Lead us not into temptation,' stretch out your arms in front of you and hold your hands up. Then swiftly open your arms out sideways as you say, 'Deliver us from evil.'

Lift one arm above your head as you say, 'For thine is the kingdom,' and lift the other as you say, 'the power and the glory'. Circle your arms as you did for 'earth' earlier each time you say 'ever'. Bring your hands into a praying position, with your palms and fingers touching, in front of your chest, and bow your head as you say, 'Amen'.

Servanthood

Tony Horsfall

Introduction

*They tell how you turned to God from idols to serve the living
and true God.*

1 THESSALONIANS 1:9 (NIV 1984)

Servanthood is not a word that my computer wants to recognise. Each
time I use the word it is underlined in red, and no alternative is given.
But it *is* a word, and I am not the only one who uses it! Servanthood is
the state of being a servant; the attitude of mind, disposition of heart,
and daily practice of someone who serves, and it is a word that aptly
describes the chosen lifestyle of those who follow Jesus.

We are reminded, in this summary description of the conversion of
the Thessalonians, of the dramatic change of allegiance that takes place
when a person turns to Christ—from a life centred on oneself (there is
no idol as powerful as the human ego) to a life of service to God. It
is this life of servanthood that we are going to explore over the next
two weeks, and we will be doing so in order to understand why we
serve, to be refreshed in the midst of our serving and perhaps to be
challenged to new expressions of service in the future.

Think about your journey of faith. From what ways of behaving and
living have you turned away? And how does the notion of servanthood
fit with your understanding of what it means to be a follower of Jesus?

The downward way of Jesus

Philippians 2:5–11

This is surely one of the most beautiful passages in the whole of scripture. It seems to have been an early Christian hymn focusing on the person and work of Christ. Whatever its origin, Paul uses these wonderfully poetic words to encourage the believers at Philippi towards unity among themselves, and into the development of a humble servant attitude like that of Christ himself.

Here we have what is often called 'the downward way of Jesus' because it describes his coming into the world and the sacrifice that he made to become one of us. For this to happen three things were necessary:

Christ had *the mind* (attitude, disposition) of a servant from the very beginning, not clinging to the rights and privileges that he had in heaven, but letting go of these (emptying himself) so that he might enter our world (vv. 6–7).

Christ took *the form* of a servant, being born as a baby and submitting himself to all the laws of human growth and development. He became exactly like us so that he could understand us and meet our need (vv. 7–8).

Christ expressed *the behaviour* of a servant, putting the needs of others before his own. For him this meant becoming obedient to the Father's will and dying for us on the cross (v. 8).

In all this Christ demonstrated the true character of a servant, namely love for others, humility of heart and mind, and a radical obedience in serving the Father. As a result, he has now been raised to the place of highest honour and authority at the Father's right hand (vv. 9–11) and declared to be Lord of all. This exaltation was made possible by his prior humiliation.

So what does this have to say to us?

Firstly, that if Jesus became a servant, we should follow his example, and honour and respect servanthood.

Secondly, that we should be prepared to walk the downward path, seeking not power, success or wealth, but being willing to serve wherever God places us and under whatever circumstances he chooses.

Thirdly, that we should cultivate in our lives the virtues of love, humility and obedience so that we may become humble servants of a humble God.

Take time to meditate on this beautiful picture of the servant king. Let your thoughts turn naturally to worship and wonder before the great mysteries of the incarnation and sacrificial death of Jesus. Perhaps craft a prayer as your response.

Find the words and, if possible, the music to 'The Servant King' by Graham Kendrick (© 1983 Thankyou Music), and savour them again in the light of this passage of scripture.

Truth be told

Here is a poem written as a response to Philippians 2:5–11, expressing the challenge I feel personally as I reflect on the 'downward way' of Jesus. If I am really honest with myself, I admire his example but struggle to follow it. As you read it through, think about the challenges you face in following Jesus. Why not write a verse yourself or even your own poem of honest response?

> *We sing your praise, O servant King,*
> *And marvel at your humble birth,*
> *Yet are we willing, truth be told,*
> *To walk that downward way ourselves*
> *And lay aside our earthly crowns?*

You came to us in hiddenness,
No fanfare for the Lowly One,
Yet are we willing, truth be told,
To shun the limelight, step aside,
And let your glory clearly shine?

You touched the leper, healed the blind,
And gathered children on your knee,
Yet are we willing, truth be told,
To serve the poor, the weak, the sick,
And go where unmet need is found?

You gave yourself to break sin's curse,
A life poured out upon the cross,
Yet are we willing, truth be told,
To offer up our gifts, our gold,
And spend our lives in serving you?

O Master whom I love so dear,
Help me to yield myself complete,
And make me willing, truth be told,
To follow where your footsteps lead,
With servant heart, and willing hands.

The true servant

Isaiah 42:1–9

Biblical scholars identify four 'servant songs' in Isaiah (42:1–9, 49:1–6, 50:4–9, 52:13—53:12), all of which speak in beautiful poetic language about an unnamed servant figure who will faithfully carry out the will of God. There has been much debate as to the identity of this person, which may refer to Isaiah himself or occasionally the people of Israel. However, the only person who truly fits the description given by the prophet is Jesus Christ, the true servant.

Matthew, who wrote his Gospel with Jewish readers in mind, was quick to make this connection. In a summary description of the ministry of Jesus, the converted tax collector is at pains to point out that this all happened to fulfil what was spoken through Isaiah, and then goes on to quote a huge chunk of the first servant song (Matthew 12:15–21 and Isaiah 42:1–4).

There seems little doubt that Jesus lived his earthly life with the consciousness of being the true servant of God. He came as one sent by the Father, to do the Father's will, and in this he delighted. So here in this first servant song we have a portrait of Jesus.

His *identity* and *calling* are made clear in verse 1. He is the one whom God has chosen to do his will, and in whom he delights. His task is to bring justice to the nations, and this he will do in the power of the Spirit. 'Justice' speaks of his work on the cross as the suffering servant, where he fulfils the law's just demands by offering himself as a sacrifice for sin; and in bringing the liberating rule of the kingdom of God to bear on the social issues of his day.

The *character* of the servant is described in verses 2–4. He will minister in humility, not pride, refusing to draw attention to himself. He will treat people with gentleness, not harshness, refusing to abuse his power. He will serve in faithfulness, refusing to quit when the way is hard.

Throughout his ministry the servant will be upheld by God (vv. 5–7), and his *confidence* is based on the word of God, who promises to be with him, to keep him, and to make him to be all that his task will require. He will bring into being a new way of relating to God (a new covenant), characterised by giving understanding (blind eyes opened), bringing liberty (captives freed), and offering hope (release from darkness). Throughout, the *attentiveness* of the servant (verses 8–9) remains constant, listening for any fresh word from the Lord.

This portrait of Jesus, the true servant, becomes the pattern for those whom he calls to follow in his steps. As the model for each of us, he has given us an example of servanthood. That which he began during his earthly life now continues through the life of his people today.

Read through Isaiah 42:1–9 and think about the ways in which Jesus fulfilled these words of Isaiah. You might find it helpful to imagine Jesus pausing at the height of his ministry to take time out with the Father, and hearing the Father speak to him through these words. Which statements have already happened and which are still to come? Stay and worship this Jesus. What do you appreciate about him? What causes you to worship him?

Read through the passage a second time, now applying it to yourself as you seek to walk in his steps. You might imagine the Father saying these same words to you. Which do you accept? Which are too 'high' for you? What challenges you? What encourages you?

Servant prayer

Here is a prayer written to be used meditatively as you respond to the call to servanthood. Don't be afraid to change it in order to make it your own, or even to use it as an inspiration to craft your own 'servant prayer'.

Lord, give me the form of a servant:
A lowly mind that does not think itself too grand;
A willing heart that does not shun hard work;
A watchful eye that does not fail to notice need;
A listening ear that does not miss your call;
A gentle touch that does not further hurt the weak;
A steady walk that does not falter under strain.
May I be always:
Motivated by love,

Angered by injustice,
Softened by suffering,
Energised by faith,
Strengthened by hope,
Governed by righteousness,
Sustained by grace.

Not to be served but to serve

Mark 10:35–45

The Gospel writers show no embarrassment in painting a picture of the disciples as they really were, making no attempt to hide their failings or gloss over their shortcomings. Here we find them squabbling about positions of power and influence in the coming kingdom. It is a sad but honest portrayal of human pride and ambition.

Jesus uses the altercation as an opportunity to teach them about the marks of true leadership. Yes, it may be among the Gentiles that leadership is seen as a way to gain power and prestige, and it may be that the leadership style they saw around them was exploitative and abusive, but it will not be like that among his followers: 'Not so with you,' says the Master (v. 43).

Leadership in the Christian community will be *servant* leadership (v. 43), characterised by humility and the absence of domination. Here the desire to serve will come first, and leadership will be a way of expressing servanthood towards the people of God.

It could never be anything less when we consider that the true Leader of the Christian community came as a servant, not demanding that he be served by others but rather willingly offering himself to meet their needs. The cross is the great example of servanthood, for there Jesus, as the suffering servant (Isaiah 52:13—53:12), gave himself completely for the sins of the world, paying the price that would set free those who were enslaved by sin. This act of total selfless love remains both the inspiration and foundation for all forms of Christian ministry today.

What, then, does it mean to be a servant leader? It means that in whatever way or at whatever level we exercise leadership, we do so with the interests of those we lead as our prime concern. Peter puts it well in his first epistle as he writes to his fellow elders: 'Be shepherds of God's flock that is under your care, serving as overseers—not because you must, but because you are willing, as God wants you to be; not greedy for money, but eager to serve; not lording it over those entrusted to you, but being examples to the flock' (1 Peter 5:2–3). No contemporary leadership manual could express it any better than this.

Pray for those you know in leadership, that they may have servant hearts and, while clear in their leadership, will not fall into the trap of dominating those they lead. When you see good leadership in operation, appreciate those who provide it by encouraging them.

If you are a leader, review your own leadership style. Ask for feedback from one or two honest and respected friends or colleagues.

Read Isaiah 52:13—53:12 again, and think about the connection between leadership and the cross.

Service with a smile

Think of very practical ways in which you might express your servant-hood towards God, towards your fellow believers, and towards your community. Some suggestions might include:

• Plan a Quiet Day so that you can be alone with God.
• Take part in a church prayer meeting or get involved in the prayer ministry of your church.
• Intentionally think about how God may want you to serve him, or pray about it, asking God: 'What would you have me do?'

- Find a practical way of helping out at church. Ask for guidance if you are uncertain.
- Visit a church member who is lonely, housebound or in hospital.
- Use the spiritual gifts that God has given you to encourage others.
- Be aware of any neighbours who may need a lift to the shops, help with the garden or simply a friendly chat, and do something about it.
- Find out which community groups are active locally and get involved—for example, food bank, debt counselling, charity shop.
- Get involved with a mission agency, or in supporting and praying for an overseas mission partner or family.
- Wherever you are, seek to be friendly and ready to offer a helping hand.

Meditation on Romans 12:11

Never be lacking in zeal, but keep your spiritual fervour, serving the Lord.
ROMANS 12:11

Spend some time meditating on this verse of scripture. Perhaps commit it to memory first of all and then turn it over in your mind, asking the Holy Spirit to unlock its meaning to you and to apply it to your life right now.

Try to answer these two questions in particular:

What robs you of spiritual fervour and diminishes your zeal?

How can you be refreshed and renewed in your service of God?

Turn your thoughts into prayer, and perhaps write down your response.

Servants or friends?

'I no longer call you servants, because a servant does not know his master's business. Instead, I have called you friends, for everything that I learned from my Father I have made known to you.'
JOHN 15:15

It may be that these thoughts on servanthood are spurring you towards action, or that they are confirming you in your already active life of serving others. Either way, I wish to sound a note of caution based on the words of Jesus to his disciples.

The caution is this: servanthood is not the only metaphor for the Christian life, nor indeed the most important. The priority for the follower of Jesus is friendship, expressed through intimacy with the Master.

The great danger in encouraging people to adopt a servant lifestyle is that we send them scurrying into hyperactivity, which eventually leads to burnout or to a frenetic show of busyness that draws them away from relationship with Jesus.

In the words given here, Jesus is reminding his disciples that their activity should flow out of their intimacy with him. Friendship on his part will be demonstrated as he lays down his life for them; on their part as they respond in obedience to his commands. What brings these two components together is that the disciples take time to be with him, to listen to his voice, and then act in accordance with his directions. What this means is that intimacy with Jesus provides the basis for activity on behalf of Jesus.

As we spend time in worship, prayer and meditation, we begin to understand more of his will and purpose. As we allow the Holy Spirit to speak to us and set ourselves to listen to his voice, we will have a greater sense of discernment as to what it is we should be doing. When we take time to review our activities before God, we will have a clearer grasp of our priorities.

There is need all around us, and if we respond to need alone we will quickly be overwhelmed. We must be about the Master's business, not implementing good ideas, copying others or impulsively following every possibility.

Remember that above all the Master loves you for who you are, not for what you do. He desires to be your friend and to share his heart with you. Make sure you have enough time to enjoy his presence.

Take a moment to think about your lifestyle. Take the last 24 hours. When did you spend time doing things for God, and when did you spend time with God? What was the balance between the two? Are you so busy doing things *for* God that you have little opportunity to spend time *with* God? How could you redress any imbalance you might discover? Imagine the next 24 hours. What would they look like if you were to spend more time with Jesus?

Receiving help

Carry each other's burdens, and in this way you will fulfil the law of Christ.
GALATIANS 6:2

Many people reading this will have little problem in being one who serves others. Indeed, for some of us the role of 'helper' comes naturally and easily, almost as an automatic response. It is the way we are, perhaps the way we have been brought up; certainly what we might consider the Christian thing to do. Where we do have difficulty, though, is in receiving help.

If we are honest, taking the role of helper can provide us with a safe hiding place. When we are always the one giving out to others, we never have to acknowledge our own need or place ourselves in the vulnerable position of receiving help from others. We may unconsciously see asking for help as a weakness or failure on our part, when in fact it is part and parcel of being human and the way authentic fellowship is both created and expressed. Unrecognised pride may prevent us from allowing others to show Christ's love to us.

One of the most popular hymns in recent years is Richard Gillard's 'The Servant Song' (© 1977 Scripture in Song), which speaks poignantly about how we can serve one another as God's people, encouraging each other on our pilgrim journey by sharing the load together. Perceptively, Gillard saw that receiving help was difficult for some people, and his hymn contains the prayer that, as well as serving others, we will have the grace to allow others to be our servant too.

All of us will have moments in our lives when we need help. We cannot always be the strong one, and sometimes we must swallow our pride and allow others to come close enough to serve us through their love and care.

If possible, track down the words of 'The Servant Song' or, better still, a recording of the song itself. Enjoy listening to these finely crafted words, and let them speak to you about the essence of true Christian fellowship—serving one another in love. If you use the internet, you will be able to find the words through a search engine, and sung versions on YouTube.

Give thanks to God for times when he has used you to help others, and for the strength and grace he gives you day by day.

Consider whether or not you allow others to get close enough in times of need. Do not be afraid to ask for help if you need it, now or in the future. It is not a sign of weakness or failure, but of genuine maturity.

Prayer of Examen

The Prayer of Examen is simply a review of the day. Why not follow this particular spiritual discipline as you follow through the theme of servanthood? Each evening you could ask yourself:

Where has God been in my day today?

When did I receive the service of another person—for example, in my family, among my friends, through my work colleagues, at church, in the ordinary events of my life? Did anyone help me, care for me, use their abilities on my behalf, put themselves out for me? Did I refuse to be helped or struggle to allow others to serve me?

Give thanks for each person, recognising that God came to you through these individuals.

Next, reflect on the ways in which you had the opportunity to serve other people—in your family, among your friends and colleagues, at church or in the ordinary events of your life. What did you do? How did it feel? Did you miss opportunities to serve? If so, why was that?

Give thanks for the way God has used you, for the privilege of serving. Ask that the servant heart will be even more fully formed within you tomorrow.

Imaginative Bible meditation

The story of how Jesus washed the feet of his disciples is a familiar one. Read through the passage in John's Gospel again (13:2–11) to remind yourself of what happened. When you feel at home in the passage, use your imagination to enter into the story.

Picture the room. What can you see, hear and smell? Who is in the room? Where are you? You might become one of the main characters, such as Peter, or you might be standing at the edge. Notice where you are and where Jesus is.

Visualise the moment when Jesus takes the bowl and the towel, and begins to disrobe so that he can fulfil the role of an ordinary household servant. How do you feel about that? What does it communicate to you?

Watch as he begins to approach the disciples one by one and to wash their feet. What do you think about this and about them? And how are you feeling as your turn approaches?

Peter hesitated at first and would not allow Jesus to wash his feet. Why do you think this was? As Jesus approaches, be aware of any resistance in you to Jesus' washing your feet. Are there aspects of your life that you would like him to wash and cleanse, or any areas you don't want him to touch? Jesus begins to wash your feet. Feel the soft warmth of the water, the cleansing of the soap and then the gentle rubbing of the towel. Feel his strong carpenter's hands holding your feet, massaging your toes. What do you sense? Listen for his word to you. What does Jesus say to you? How do you respond? Stay with Jesus and talk to him.

When you are ready, leave the scene. You might like to reflect on some of the things you noticed or felt during the exercise.

If you find it helpful, write down your response.

Julian of Norwich

Andrea Skevington

Seeing the love of God

'In this vision there are many comforting and very moving words for all those who wish to be lovers of Christ.'

INTRODUCTION TO SHORT TEXT

Julian of Norwich is something of an enigma. We know little of her life: even the name by which we call her is not her own. It is taken from the Church of St Julian in Norwich where she had her cell. But her writing gives us a fascinating window into her inner life. Her *Revelations of Divine Love* is the first book written in English by a woman, and Rowan Williams has said that it 'may well be the most important work of Christian reflection in the English language' (see www.christianitytoday.com/ct/2010/august/13.51.html).

For the modern reader, it contains an intriguing mixture of profound insight and unsettling images. It helps to see the work in the context of its time. We believe that Julian lived between 1342 and c. 1416, a dark and turbulent period of English history. She lived through the Black Death, which cut Norwich's population by about a third, the Hundred Years' War, and the Peasants' Revolt with the executions outside Norwich Cathedral that followed. Many believed these were signs of God's wrath. The Church responded by preaching on sin and hell fire, the wickedness of mankind and the corruption of the earth. In the light of this, Julian's insights into the unending and unquenchable love of God, and his delight in all that he made, are truly remarkable.

So, too, is her courage in sharing them in an age when women could be burned to death as heretics or witches.

By her own account, the turning points in her life were a simple prayer, an illness that took her close to death, and a series of 16 'showings' or visions that accompanied it.

> 'I asked for three graces of God's gift. The first was vivid perception of Christ's Passion, the second was bodily sickness, and the third was for God to give me three wounds... that is to say, the wound of contrition, the wound of compassion and the wound of an earnest longing for God... The first two of the longings just mentioned... passed from my mind, and the third stayed with me continually.'
> JULIAN OF NORWICH, *REVELATIONS OF DIVINE LOVE*, PENGUIN CLASSICS, 1998, SHORT TEXT, CHAPTER 1

> 'And when I was thirty and a half years old, God sent me a bodily sickness in which I lay for three days and three nights; and on the fourth night I received all the rites of Holy Church and did not believe that I would live until morning... those who were with me sent for the parson, my parish priest, to be present at my death... "Daughter, I have brought you the image of your Saviour. Look upon it and be comforted."'
> SHORT TEXT, CHAPTER 2

As she looked on that image, the 'showings' began. Later, as an anchorite or solitary contemplative, she wrote of her experience (Short Text) and her reflections on it (Long Text).

Prayer and reflection: look again at Julian's prayer—what she wanted of God. Consider the three wounds: of sorrow for sin, compassion, and the earnest longing for God. How much do we long for God? Ask God to give you a deep hunger for him as we enter on this series of meditations.

Read Psalm 63:1–8, making it your own prayer.

Meditation

'So I saw and understood that our faith is our light in our night, which light is God, our endless day.'
JULIAN OF NORWICH: *SHOWINGS*, TRANSLATED BY EDMUND COLLEDGE AND JAMES WALK, PAULIST PRESS, 1978, QUOTED IN GLORIA DURKA, *PRAYING WITH JULIAN OF NORWICH*, SAINT MARY'S PRESS, 1989

Find a quiet place. You may wish to draw the curtains or dim the lights. Now light a candle and ask Jesus to show you the power of the light of the world in the darkness.

Become aware of your breathing, slow and gentle, and take time to read Luke 23:44–49. Notice how those who knew Jesus stayed. So stay now, at the foot of the cross, and ask Jesus for an insight into the depth of his love.

Julian's first showing was looking into Christ's face on the cross. This was where her journey began.

'And I suddenly saw the red blood trickling down from under the crown of thorns, all hot, freshly, plentifully and vividly, just as I imagined it was at the moment when the crown of thorns was thrust on to his blessed head—he who was both God and man, the same who suffered for me.'
SHORT TEXT, CHAPTER 3

'Very happily our Lord… said these words: "Look how much I loved you… My child… see here how I let my side be opened, and my heart be riven in two, and all the blood and water that was within flow out. And this makes me happy, and I want it to make you happy."'
SHORT TEXT, CHAPTER 13

Read the Luke passage again, out loud if you can, pausing to offer up prayers of thanksgiving.

Creative response

'And therefore with his grace and his help we may stand and gaze at him in the spirit, with unending amazement at this high, surpassing, inestimable love that almighty God has for us in his goodness.'

LONG TEXT, CHAPTER 6

Re-read the Luke passage (Luke 23:44–49), and think how you could respond creatively to the immeasurable love of Jesus. Here are some suggestions:

Music: listen to some of the great music that has been written on this theme, such as Bach's *St Matthew Passion*, hymns or contemporary worship songs. Lose yourself in the power of the music. Maybe you could dance.

The crown of thorns: if you have access to thorny stems, you could make a crown of thorns—with care—imagining what it meant to Jesus to wear it. Alternatively, you might like to draw a representation of the crown of thorns, or of the darkness and pain of that moment when Jesus was crowned with such a false crown.

The curtain: find an old sheet or a large sheet of paper. As you think about the curtain of the Holy of Holies, tear it from top to bottom, remembering what it represents: the anguish of the father, tearing his clothes; the joy of the father, making a way for all to enter in.

Writing: Julian wrote Jesus' words to her as she saw this showing. Ask what Jesus would say to you, personally, as you stay at the foot of the cross. Write it down. You could start with some words of scripture.

A vision of love

'Let him lead me to the banquet hall, and let his banner over me be love.'
SONG OF SONGS 2:4 (NIV)

In an age when the Church preached God's wrath and judgment, Julian's vision of the love of God is remarkable. Take some time to pray through these words.

'I saw that for us he is everything that is good and comforting and helpful. He is our clothing, wrapping and enveloping us for love, embracing us and guiding us in all things, hanging about us in tender love, so that he can never leave us. And so in this vision, as I understand it, I saw truly that he is every-thing that is good for us.'
SHORT TEXT, CHAPTER 4

'And I, contemplating all this through his grace, saw that his love for our souls is so strong that he chose the pain willingly and eagerly, and suffered it meekly and was well pleased to do so.'
LONG TEXT, CHAPTER 21

See also these verses: Ephesians 1:4–10, 18–20; John 3:16–17; 1 John 4:16–17.

You could use some of the words above to commit to heart and to say during the day. Write a prayer to remember, taking Psalm 118 as a model, adding 'His love endures forever' to the end of each phrase.

The three windows

After her illness, Julian spent many years as an anchoress attached to a church in Norwich. The church is near the castle and the quayside, so she was not isolated. Her anchorhold, a sparse room about ten foot square, had three windows: one into the church, so that she could participate in services, one for a maid to care for her, and one on to the highway to speak to people who came for advice. Her life was a mix of contemplation and participation, of isolation and involvement.

Let us consider the importance of windows.

Begin by sitting where you can look out of a window. Try to still your inner life and truly look. You could draw or describe what you see. Ask God to speak to you through what you see. R.S. Thomas' poem 'The View from the Window' might help.

Now, think of Julian's window into the church. She participated in Mass through this window—a reminder of Jesus' great love, and his command that we should love each other.

> 'But in truth, I am moved to tell you about it by love, for I wish God to be known and my fellow Christians helped, as I wish to be helped myself, so that sin shall be more hated and God more loved.'
>
> SHORT TEXT, CHAPTER 6

What would it be like to be part of your church through a window? What would you miss? Spend some time thinking and praying about your involvement with other Christians, asking God for the capacity to love and serve (see 1 Corinthians 13).

An exercise in thankfulness

Julian's second window allowed her maids, Sara and Alice, to bring her food and water and tend to her physical needs.

In your journal, if you keep one, spend one day recording all the things you receive that you need in your life. Naturally, you will list what you eat and drink, but think about other things that help you and serve you. Now think about the people who provide them and list them alongside. You could take one particular person, for example, a coffee grower or a police officer, and find out more about their life.
Go through your list, giving thanks for all you receive.

> *When a Samaritan woman came to draw water, Jesus said to her, 'Will you give me a drink?'*
> JOHN 4:7

The busy highway

Julian's third window opened on to the road near the river quay: a busy highway. It seems that many people stopped to ask for her advice and prayers. Hunger, plague and sorrow visited her through the people. She responded with God's peace.

> 'So I saw that God is our true peace; and he is our safe protector when we ourselves are in disquiet, and he constantly works to bring us into endless peace.'
> JULIAN OF NORWICH: *SHOWINGS*, QUOTED IN *PRAYING WITH JULIAN OF NORWICH*

Consider the windows in your life that bring you into contact with suffering and distress. Newspapers and television could open windows to lives far away. How can we respond to that suffering?

Think too of the windows into the suffering of those known to you: conversations, letters, the internet. Pray that God's endless peace will flow through all disquiet.

Although Julian sought quiet to pray, she never saw her spirituality as a personal quest. Rather, she drew closer to Jesus, who walked on this earth to heal, help and save. How do we balance the need for time spent experiencing God's love with time spent loving God's hurting world? Write down any conflicts you feel, seeing if solutions emerge.

Read Mark 1:35–38.

The hazelnut

'In this vision he also showed a little thing, the size of a hazel-nut in the palm of my hand, and it was as round as a ball.
I looked at it with my mind's eye and thought, "What can this be?" And the answer came to me, "It is all that is made."
I wondered how it could last, for it was so small I thought it might suddenly have disappeared. And the answer in my mind was, "It lasts and will last forever because God loves it; and everything exists in the same way by the love of God."
In this little thing I saw three properties: the first is that God made it, the second is that God loves it, the third is that God cares for it.'

LONG TEXT, CHAPTER 5

Read these well-loved words slowly and carefully, holding in your mind anything that particularly strikes you. Thank God for his love and care.

Creative responses

Walking: If you can, go for a walk in a natural space. As you walk, repeat to yourself, 'God made it, God loves it, God cares for it.' Take in the bounty and abundance of all that you see. Respond in wonder. You may be able to gather nuts on your walk: hazels, acorns, chestnuts.

Perspectives: take a nut in your hand, as Julian did in her showing, and spend some time going through her words. Consider how small the things are that we worry about, but how great God's love for all.

Gather pictures of the wonders of the universe from different perspectives, looking at both large—the stars, the galaxies, cosmology—and small, whether it's considering quantum mechanics or looking through a microscope. Shift your perspectives on what God has made. Remember that in John 3:16, the Greek word used for 'world' is 'cosmos'.

Artwork: take crayons or paints, and spend some time drawing or painting anything that has struck you from this meditation. Be impressionistic, trying to capture the life and energy of things, rather than the details of their appearance. As you do so, try to dwell on the creative energy of God, maker, lover, sustainer of all.

Alternatively, you could make a miniature world out of clay (or use a ball), covering it with tiny pictures or the words you used on your walk. Keep it where it will help you to remember God's love.

Resting in God's love

Knowing that all things are made and sustained by God's love, we can learn to rest in that love.

'This is the reason why we do not feel complete ease in our hearts and souls: we look here for satisfaction in things which are so trivial, where there is no rest to be found, and do not know God who is almighty, all wise, all good; he is rest itself.'
LONG TEXT, CHAPTER 5

'And after this our Lord showed himself in even greater glory, it seemed to me, than when I saw him before, and from this revelation I learned that our soul will never rest until it comes to him knowing that he is the fullness of joy, of everyday and princely blessedness and the only true life.'
LONG TEXT, CHAPTER 26

Meditation

Take some time to quieten your body and mind and spirit, to rest, to lean back on God's care, calling to mind the words of Psalm 23.

Response

Write something celebrating what you love in creation, or that reflects your sense of God's care for you. Here is a simple poem I wrote, drawing from Psalm 23.

My pasture is green.
My small world, cupped in
Your hand, grows.
Today, shadows are

soft, and the sun
shimmers on clear waters.
Apples swell
on the bent branch.
I rest in the hollow of
Your palm.

Reflection

What difference does it make to you, today, to live in the certainty of God's endless care?

Intercessory prayer

God showed Julian all that was made, as if it were in the palm of her own hand. He wishes to draw us into his compassionate work of loving and caring for the world and for others. One way we do this is through prayer.

Pray for our world, remembering all you have delighted in. Consider those things that threaten creation and pray about them, too.

Remember places where there is suffering: those you saw through Julian's window. Bring all these situations before God, sure in the knowledge of his love and care.

You might like to keep a record of your prayers, to remind you to uphold people and situations before God.

End your prayers with Julian's thoughts: 'For you made the world, and you love it, and you care for it.'

On prayer

As Julian reflected on the hazelnut showing, she wrote:

> 'This showing was made to teach our souls to be wise and cling to the goodness of God. And at that point our usual way of praying came into my thoughts; how usually, because we do not understand or know about love, we pray indirectly.'
>
> LONG TEXT, CHAPTER 6

> 'Prayer unites the soul to God... And so he teaches us to pray and to have firm trust that we shall have it; for he beholds us in love, and wants to make us partners in his good will and work... The whole reason why we pray is to be united into the vision and contemplation of him to whom we pray.'
>
> JULIAN OF NORWICH: *SHOWINGS*, QUOTED IN *PRAYING WITH JULIAN OF NORWICH*

If you can, find silence and still your heart. Spend some time thinking of the goodness and love of God, and ask God to speak to you. Do not be afraid of silence. In your imagination, open yourself up to God's loving kindness.

Take time each day to find silence and stillness, making a habit of seeking quietness of spirit even in the midst of busyness.

> 'Pray earnestly even though you do not feel like praying, for it is helping you even if you do not feel it doing you good, even if you see nothing, yes, even if you think you cannot pray; for in dryness and in barrenness, in sickness and weakness, then your prayers give me great pleasure even if you feel that they are hardly pleasing to you at all.'
>
> LONG TEXT, CHAPTER 41

'Lord, teach us to pray.'
LUKE 11:1

All shall be well

'All shall be well, all shall be well, and all manner of things shall be well.'
SHORT TEXT, CHAPTER 14

Variations on these words run through Julian's writings, flowing from the certainty of God's merciful, forgiving love. They speak of the conviction that God holds all things in his care, including each one of us.

'Ah, my good Lord, how could all be well, given the great harm that has been done to humankind by sin?' … 'Since I have turned the greatest possible harm [the cross] into good, it is my will that you should know from this that I shall turn all lesser evil into good.'
SHORT TEXT, CHAPTER 14

Julian's writings show great consciousness of sin, and the harm it can do. She was fully aware of the havoc evil wreaks in the world, and developed a habit of mind that saw God's love as greater than all.

Confession and forgiveness

As we wish to live in unity with God, we need to be forgiven for our wrongs, and forgive the wrongs done to us. As you pray this prayer, be specific: apply it to your life.

Most merciful God,
we know that we have sinned,
and that sin is a sharp scourge
that wounds and wrecks your image in us,
that wrecks our hope, and our love for each other.
Your love is so great, and ours can be so thin and small.
Our thoughts, our words and deeds have been unworthy of you.
We have not loved you as we should.
We have not loved each other as we should.
We have not tended creation as we should.
We are sorry. Have mercy, most merciful God,
forgive us, and by the power and grace of
your Spirit, renew and restore us,
so that we may live as your friends,
walking in your garden,
overflowing with your love. Amen

Know that you are forgiven:

> 'He did not say, "You shall not be tormented, you shall not be troubled, you shall not be grieved," but he said, "You shall not be overcome."'
>
> SHORT TEXT, CHAPTER 22

Sometimes we find it hard to forgive those who have tormented, troubled and grieved us. We can keep records of the wrongs against us.

Take some time bringing those who have hurt you before God, praying that you will be able to forgive, to let go of the hurt. Trust God to deal with the situation and ask for the grace to bless the people involved.

If there is one situation that has been particularly difficult, why not write it down and offer it to God. Tear up the paper slowly and deliberately, saying that you will let the situation go and not carry the burden of it any longer. You could burn the shredded paper. If the situation is still burdensome, you might like to talk it through with a wise friend or counsellor.

Creative response

Many have memorised 'All shall be well', or other significant words Julian wrote, using them as the basis for prayer and meditation throughout the day. You might like to make something to help you remember. Here are some suggestions:

- A bookmark written as beautifully as you can, illustrated with hazelnuts, catkins or leaves. You could take prints of the leaves with paint or inks.
- A small card to pin by your bed, or have at your desk, illustrated in the same way.
- Embroidery: if you embroider, you could use that skill to make something beautiful.
- Photography: take photographs, adding the words. You could print them out to share.
- Clay: you can buy air-drying clay, which you could inscribe with a sharp skewer or knife, using these words. You could impress a hazel leaf into the clay. If you have a ceramics café nearby, you could decorate a mug or a plate, ringing it with the words, to use daily.

The psalmists often recalled times when God had helped his people in the past, to encourage them to pray about current difficulties. You could write a prayer, giving thanks for answered prayer in your own life, using Julian's words 'all shall be well' as a refrain. Use this prayer when you are feeling troubled or doubting.

The story of Ruth

Sally Welch

An everyday story

For over 60 years, *The Archers*—originally described as 'an everyday story of country folk', now 'a contemporary drama in a rural setting'—has told of the lives and events of a group of people living in a rural community. In a way, there can be no better description of the book of Ruth than 'an everyday story of country folk'. In this book we learn what it was like to live in the countryside in Old Testament times. Struggles for food, family loyalties and difficult life-changing decisions all take place against a backdrop of seedtime and harvest, hard work and celebration. Yet if the book were no more than that, it would not speak to us today. But, just like *The Archers*, it can also be described as 'a contemporary drama in a rural setting', because the issues it deals with and the relationship each character has with God still have a great deal to teach us, not just about God but about ourselves, even after all these years.

Ruth 1:19–22

The book of Ruth has been described as the only book in the Bible in which all the characters behave themselves! However, at the beginning, it does not seem as if this will be so. We are introduced first to Naomi, whose husband and sons have died. With nothing to look forward to, she is resigned to a lonely, poverty-stricken life, and decides to return to her home country.

On her return, some women greet Naomi by name. She tells them that she should no longer be called Naomi, meaning 'pleasant', but Mara, which means 'bitter', because of the action of the Lord against her. The deaths of her husband and two sons have left Naomi feeling that life has nothing more to offer her. Death was much to be feared in the Old Testament—the shadowy underworld of *Sheol*, the place of the dead, was a place of darkness and terror. The whole of Naomi's future had been snatched from her: to see not one child but two children die is a heart-rending affair. She has every right to be bitter. However, Naomi's character and her faith in God are stronger than that, and she will not give in to her despair. Even in the Old Testament there is a belief that God is lord of life and death. In Psalm 139 we are reminded that even if the psalmist makes his bed in *Sheol* itself, 'you are there' (v. 8, NIV)—nowhere in heaven or earth is God absent. So even in the midst of her sorrow, Naomi is confident in her belief in an all-loving creator God. What is more, she is sure that God can handle her anger towards him. She cannot resist telling him how she feels about her situation, but that too is a sign of the truthfulness of her relationship with him. For Naomi, nothing is hidden from God.

Look back at the times when you have suffered. Did you cry out to God in anger, or did you distance yourself from him? How has your relationship with God changed and developed through periods of unhappiness in your life—was your faith strengthened or did your doubt increase? If you wish, cry out to him in anger. Do not be afraid, because God knows the secrets of our hearts and is present even when we try to shut him out. Remember that we have the promise of the resurrection to sustain us; the belief that to die is not merely to sink into oblivion or to wander among the shadows in a terror-filled place, but to enjoy eternal fellowship with Christ. Our destination is a place where all pain and suffering have ceased and our tears are wiped away by God himself.

Naomi—a widow

Being a woman in Old Testament times was hard work. Women got married at a very young age and took on a great many tasks within the family. They were responsible for fetching water, looking after the fires, making bread, cooking and serving meals, cleaning the home, making and mending clothes and tending the domestic animals. In rural areas they would also be called upon to help with agricultural tasks at particular times of year. Despite these responsibilities, a wife was numbered among her husband's possessions and could be divorced very easily. The actions of Jesus in giving women time and attention and respecting their opinions were truly radical. Yet although women carried little weight in society as a whole, they were responsible for the family and as such were generally respected, especially if they bore a male child, ensuring the continuation of the family line. It is because of this that so much significance is attached to the pain and sorrow of childless women, such as Abraham's wife Sarah and Samuel's mother Hannah, and to their joy when they did finally give birth to boys. However, women could not inherit land or property—all their security was vested in their husbands, whose death would leave them in a very difficult position. If they could, they would often go to live with their sons, who took on responsibility for their wellbeing, but if there were no sons, poverty and isolation threatened. The very word 'widow' in Hebrew carries with it connotations of loneliness and being abandoned.

In our society, the situation of widows may not be as bleak as that of Naomi and her daughters-in-law. However, there are still people who are isolated from society by financial hardship, bereavement, illness, or simply a move to a new and unfamiliar place. Throughout the Bible we are told that God cares for the friendless, and we are shown how he can work through them—consider the widow who feeds Elijah during a time of famine (1 Kings 17) or the widow whose son is brought back from the dead by Jesus (Luke 7). As we seek to walk more closely with

God, we need to remain aware of the lost and friendless within our community and reach out a loving hand towards them in their need.

Meditation

Ruth 4:14–15

Consider a patchwork quilt—a bed cover made from lots of different pieces of material pieced together to form a large piece of fabric. Patchwork was originally done by poorer members of society, who could not afford to throw away torn or worn-out garments. Instead, they took them apart and saved the less worn pieces. Then they would stitch together the remnants of these old garments and create something new, something whole, something beautiful. These quilts would transform an ordinary bed or chair into a work of art, filling the room with colour and pattern.

Our lives too are like a patchwork quilt, made of episodes of laughter and sorrow, stitched together with God's love. With God's grace, from the sorrow and pain of parts of our lives the beautiful and good can emerge—insights gained, relationships deepened, sympathies enlarged. These can be put together to form a new creation in God's image, full of truth and beauty. Just as well-made patchwork can brighten the surroundings in which it is placed, so our lives, pieced together with love and faith from fragments of good and bad, joy and sorrow, can enrich the lives of those around us.

Looking back on her life, Naomi must have marvelled at how both good and ill, suffering and rejoicing, could combine to form part of God's plan. So it is with all our lives. Take some time to look back over your life, at the good times and the bad, and consider how they flow into and out of each other. Remember that your whole life is precious to God and a thing of great beauty. You might like to draw some patchwork pieces and label them for the different times in your life, colouring them to make a thing of beauty, and offering each one to God. Or you could cut out pieces of paper or fabric and place them together as a patchwork, thinking of different times in your life. Watch how they fit together to make a beautiful whole.

A spiritual timeline

Draw your 'spiritual timeline'. Find a large piece of paper and some coloured pens or pencils, as many as you can. Draw a horizontal line at the foot of the page and mark it off in years from birth up to your present age. Draw a vertical line up from this line at the left-hand side of the paper. At the top of this line, write 'at one with God', and at the bottom, 'completely absent from God'. Now, beginning with your first realisation of God's action in your life, chart your spiritual ups and downs, relating them to instances in your life. So, for example, your conscious spiritual journey with God may have begun while you were listening to Bible stories in Sunday school, or when you were at college, or during some occasion of extreme suffering. You might have felt closer to God when something good happened or something bad. Try and map this out for your whole life.

Once this is complete, reflect on your spiritual timeline. Do you feel closer to God when things are going well or badly? Do you forget God in moments of extreme emotion? Are there passages from the Bible that help you to understand this better? Does the bitterness of Naomi ring true for some moments in your life? Can you look back and see points of learning or understanding that have arisen out of a crisis or significant event? Reflect on the fact that some suffering can open us to deeper dimensions of the spiritual life. Sometimes we can discern good out of what has happened, sometimes not. Sometimes pain can be the pathway to growth and maturity of character; sometimes it must remain a mystery.

Ruth's promise

Ruth 1:16–17

Although the book of Ruth begins with Naomi's story, the action that determines the course of the book is Ruth's response to the faith of her mother-in-law. Ruth decides to follow an elderly, frail woman into unknown territory, to learn more about the God who guides her and loves her.

This reading, often used in marriage services, contains a beautiful promise that is at the heart of a life committed to the wellbeing of another. Ruth puts into words a resolution to give her life in the service of Naomi. She demonstrates an unselfish love, fuelled by determination and guided by an awareness of something greater than herself. For at the heart of Ruth's promise to share Naomi's life and frighteningly uncertain future is a deep resolution to share Naomi's God. Ruth is setting off on a journey with a woman who is not from her country, whom she loves but whose tie to her has been broken by death. She is travelling to a land she has never seen and which is inhabited by enemies of her people. She has denied herself everything—the love of her family, the protection of her community, all that is familiar and known—in order to share Naomi's life and her God. We must marvel at Ruth's sensitivity to the Spirit within her, at the grace of God in using not only the children of Israel but all his people to move forward his purposes for the world.

Most of all, we must take to heart the strength of Naomi's faith that she demonstrated such an example of belief and trust to Ruth. Just as God used the experience and faith of Naomi to point Ruth towards himself, so he wants to use us. Are our lives lived in such a way that people seeing our lives express the desire to get to know our God? Does our life impel others to say with Ruth, 'your people will be my people and your God will be my God' (v. 16)?

We can begin with the people in our family and our community.

Commit yourself to praying for them and their wellbeing, asking for God's help in dealing with those people you find difficult or hurtful. Do not stop at prayers alone—small deeds of thoughtful kindness can make a huge difference to those around us. They do not have to be much—perhaps a kind word or a note of appreciation. It will not take long for this spirit of loving kindness to grow within us and to be recognised and reciprocated by others in our community.

Meditation

Ruth 4:5–9

Imagine what it must have been like to be Ruth, sent by Naomi, whom she deeply loves and respects, to ask Boaz to look after them. How much courage and faith must she have needed! Use the following passage to try and put yourself in Ruth's place.

It is dark, very dark outside. The hour is late and the settlement is quiet except for the occasional yelping of a wild dog or the muttering of a man as he turns in his sleep. All sleep deeply, for the harvest has been good and the celebrations correspondingly joyful.

Only two people are awake, and they stand together at the doorway of a hut some distance from the big barn where the crops have been gathered. The older woman turns to the younger and hugs her, muttering encouraging words, finally kissing her on the forehead before gently pushing her out of the hut. The younger woman stumbles a little, catching her feet on a stone as her eyes adjust to the darkness. Then she moves softly across the courtyard to the looming blackness of the opening into the barn. Once, she freezes into stillness, hearing a movement in the outer darkness, where the settlement merges into the countryside. She fears discovery, but after pausing for a moment, discounts the noises and moves forward once more.

Reaching the doorway of the barn, she pauses and leans against the door post, peering intently into a blackness so deep it is like a physical barrier. It is now that she must summon up all her courage and loyalty, now that she must draw upon her love for Naomi and her faith in that woman's wisdom. She knows the vital importance of continuing the family line, she knows that only by marrying can she hope to bear the son who will ensure their livelihood, and yet she hesitates. What a huge risk she is taking, seeking to become truly a part of God's covenant family, asking to take refuge under the protection of Boaz in marriage.

Silently, she tiptoes through the sleeping bodies of the men who have drunk deeply of the harvest wine and now snore gently on the barn floor. Steadily, she makes her way to the man lying slightly apart from the others. With infinite stealth she lies down at his feet, hardly daring to breathe at the enormity of the task she is undertaking, her whole future resting on the next few moments. The man stirs as his feet touch her body. Startled, he sits up, staring bleary-eyed at the woman. 'Who are you?' he asks. She summons up all her courage, prays her most fervent prayer and answers, 'I am your servant Ruth. Spread the corner of your garment over me, since you are a kinsman-redeemer.'

Consider times in your own life when you have performed an act of courage. What did you feel? Were you aware of God's presence? Do you know others who need courage right now? What must they feel? Try to put yourself in their place, and use this insight to pray for them.

Footprints

Ruth first knew God through knowing Naomi. The way Naomi lived her life, practised her faith and demonstrated her deep and trusting relationship with God showed Ruth something of the nature and character of God. Without Naomi's example, that inner consciousness, that indwelling Spirit might not have been named by Ruth, and she might never have met her creator or the rest of the children of God.

Take some pieces of paper, preferably of different colours, and draw the outline of a foot on each of them. If you can, cut these out so that you have several footprints.

Take some time to reflect on the people through whose lives you have encountered God. They might be a Christian teacher, a fellow worker, a priest, a family member. They might be writers, journalists, hymn writers. They might have taught you about God and you might have heard their sermons, read their books. They might have shown how God acts through other people simply by the way they lived their lives. Their love for you or for others might have reflected God's love for you. Take as much time as you need, then write their names on the paper footprints. Place the footprints on the floor as if they were walking across the room.

Look at the footprints in front of you. Marvel at the many people who have helped you in your faith journey. Pray for them and pray for yourself that you too may be a footprint, showing others the way to Christ.

Prayers

Loving God, we pray that we might be like Ruth, faithful and loving. Help us to seek new ways to demonstrate love and kindness without expectation of reward. Give us the gifts of loyalty to those with whom we share our lives, of unselfish sacrifice and an obedient heart.

Faithful God, we pray that we might have the gift of faith like Naomi. Help us to see your loving action in all that happens; give us the grace to discern your purposes and to trust in their goodness. Accompany us on our journey to our true home which lies with you, and help us to travel faithfully and expectantly. May we in our lives and actions show others the way, just as we have ourselves been shown the way.

Mighty God, help us to use our power and influence for the good of others. Show us how to deal as generously as Boaz with those who seek our aid, putting their wellbeing ahead of ours and expressing your love in our dealings with all we meet. Give us a heart for the strangers and outcasts among us, that we may welcome them into our midst and share our home with them.

Father God, we thank you for the gift of your Son, who gave his life to redeem ours. He paid the price of our redemption freely and willingly, despite its great cost, and made us his children for all time. May we live as members of your family, secure in the knowledge of your love.

Boaz—kinsman redeemer

Ruth 2:12

From the beginning of chapter 2, we know that Naomi has a rich relative who is able to take care of her and Ruth, and it is important that we know that, although Naomi does not. It is not a suspense story but a work of witness to God's providence. When Ruth tells of her encounter with Boaz, Naomi is delighted, for here is a kinsman to take care of them, and it seems as if Boaz is willing to do just that, but for one final obstacle of a nearer kinsman.

When Boaz first meets Ruth he shows his faith by praying that God might reward her for her actions towards Naomi. It must be remembered that this is not a faith that is dependent on reward for good actions. Neither Boaz nor Ruth expects to earn favour by their sacrifices. Boaz's prayer for Ruth is that of a deeper reward, of something more satisfying than an increase in riches or greater physical security. Just as her loyalty to Naomi springs from her walk with God, so Ruth will benefit from her actions by a closer relationship with God. By praying for a better knowledge of God and his grace towards her, Boaz is treating Ruth as a true child of Israel—a compliment indeed.

The poetry of the final phrase is echoed in the Psalms: 'in the shadow of your wings I will take refuge, until the destroying storms pass by' (Psalm 57:1, NRSV), 'for you have been my help, and in the shadow of your wings I sing for joy' (Psalm 63:7). Boaz, mindful of all that Ruth has been through and recognising her craving for peace and security, offers this as his prayer, as yet unaware that he himself will be the answer to this prayer by providing Ruth with the shelter of his own home. We too can pray to experience that sense of refuge and security within the shadow of God's wings of love, ever mindful of our need to offer a similar peace and security to others in our turn.

Jigsaw

Ruth's life is not an easy one. Widowed young, a stranger in a foreign land, with only an elderly woman for company, did she wonder why God had treated her in such a way? She was unaware that all these actions and her responses were leading towards a greater purpose, for Ruth's son would be an ancestor of David, from whose line Jesus Christ was born. Looking back at Ruth's life, we can put it in perspective; at the time, Ruth simply had faith and prayer to sustain her.

Find a jigsaw, ideally a child's one, with few pieces, which can be quickly made. Break it up and scatter the pieces in front of you. Look at how messy the space looks, filled with scattered bits of colour and shape, making no sense, unpleasing to the eye. Pick up one piece of jigsaw. See how it gives very little idea of the whole picture. You cannot tell what the final image will look like, nor how big it is, nor what it represents.

Now build the jigsaw, fitting the pieces together slowly and carefully, appreciating how the picture gradually becomes clearer. Our lives can sometimes feel like a broken jigsaw, with jagged pieces scattered randomly, making no sense. Some of the pieces can feel ugly and painful, giving no joy, only sorrow. Sometimes, later on in our lives, incidents that were unhappy or damaging at the time can be seen to have brought goodness in their wake—a renewed relationship, a time of peace and healing. If you can identify such times, thank God for them, for both the brokenness of the initial incident and the wholeness and understanding it brought you. If there are events that still do not fit into your jigsaw of life in a way that brings meaning or understanding, pray for the faith to trust that on the last day, you will be given the grace to see your life as it is, whole and perfect in God, according to his excellent and most loving purposes for us.

Going deeper

One of the most interesting facets of the book of Ruth is the way in which the Old Testament laws are taken one step further and infused with loving sacrifice. When Ruth follows Naomi, she is taking the tradition of kinship and loyalty to its loving, logical conclusion. Here is a fragile woman, beset by hardship. Ruth accompanies her, to protect and care for her, just as she was protected by Naomi as a young bride. When Ruth gleans the leftover grain, she is taking advantage of the laws that required reapers to leave a portion of the crop to be collected by the needy. Boaz goes one step further and instructs his reapers not to collect any fallen grain.

Because God rescued the children of Israel from Egypt, as part of their covenant relationship with him they must rescue others. The relationship is deepened when it goes beyond what is merely required to become what is given in loving recognition of common humanity. However, despite Boaz's generosity, what Naomi and Ruth really need to survive is a redeemer, a protector of their future. As widows, their one real hope lay in marrying a second time, to provide a male child to continue the family line. Traditionally this was the role of the nearest male relative of the husband—his brother, for example. This role, known as a *levir*, Boaz is happy to take on, but there is a closer kinsman. This kinsman is unwilling to marry Ruth, however, so Boaz is free to marry her and provide her with a home, security and a future in the shape of a male child.

As Christians, we have no need for a human *levir* to rescue us and protect us. By paying the ultimate price for our freedom, Christ brings us into a new family of his children. No longer needing to rely on the unpredictable goodness of distant kinsmen, we are redeemed finally and completely through Christ's sacrifice for us. Willingly taking on the role, he has ensured our future; we can have complete faith in his saving love.

Meditation

The book of Ruth is suffused with prayer, like a golden thread running in and out of the everyday lives. Every action is illuminated with prayer; every prayer deepens a character's relationship with God. Naomi sends Orpah back to Moab with prayer: 'May the Lord grant that… you will find rest in the home of another husband' (1:9, NIV). Boaz greets his workers with prayer (2:4). As we have seen, Boaz's welcome to Ruth includes prayer (2:12), and Naomi greets Ruth's news of Boaz with prayer (2:20). Boaz responds to Ruth's brave visit with prayer (3:10); a prayer is said on the occasion of their marriage (4:11–12), and finally, Ruth's baby son is given to Naomi with prayer (4:14).

More than anything else, this book demonstrates a way of life that is rooted and grounded in prayer. Every event, both good and bad, is brought before God—even Naomi's anguished arrival in Israel involves a prayer to God, albeit an angry one. Prayer is a way of sharing our lives with the one who created them. It is a way of saying 'yes' to the purposes of God, responding to his invitation to a life rooted in faith in his providence.

Just as Ruth, Naomi and Boaz pray, unceasingly, confidently and lovingly, so we can commit ourselves to doing the same. You could pray when you meet someone for the first time—just ask God's blessing on them, like Boaz. You could bring events before God, remembering his presence and asking for his guidance. The witness of Ruth, Naomi and Boaz to God's providential care shines out across the centuries. Let us pray in our turn that we may be such examples to others, and that our lives of constant, faithful prayer bring us the same rewarding depth of relationship with God.

Advent (1)

Angela Ashwin

Introduction

Isaiah 40:1–11

'Comfort, O comfort my people,' says your God.
ISAIAH 40:1

The season of Advent, which literally means 'coming' or 'arrival', is spiced with anticipation and wonder. As we prepare to celebrate the coming of Christ, our prayer and worship are enriched by vivid biblical imagery such as the desert blossoming (Isaiah 35:1), the herald announcing good news from the mountain top (Isaiah 40:9), and maidens with oil lamps waiting for the bridegroom (Matthew 25:1–13). This period of preparation before Christmas first developed into an official church season in fifth-century Gaul (modern France), and over the centuries it has become a time when we remember Christ's awesome majesty, both now and in eternity. Paradoxically, we also think about the extraordinary vulnerability of the Christ-child as we ponder the implications of his birth into our dark and dangerous world.

Advent is also a time for penitence, and some churches reflect this tradition by using purple vestments and altar cloths. In the midst of all the activity and bustle of December, it is good to try to find times in which to pause and do some honest self-examination. If we feel some anxiety as we stand exposed before the light of Christ, we can also be assured that we are held in the infinite mercy and love of God: 'See, the Lord God comes with might… He will feed his flock like a shepherd; he will gather the lambs in his arms' (Isaiah 40:10–11). These and other sublime words in today's passage from Isaiah contribute to the atmosphere of hopeful expectancy that pervades these weeks. You may like to light a white candle to mark the beginning of Advent; this could also be incorporated into an Advent ring (see page 96).

Waiting and desiring

Throughout Advent there is a sense of waiting and longing for God:

> *I wait for the Lord, my soul waits, and in his word I hope; my soul waits for the Lord more than those who watch for the morning.*
> PSALM 130:5–6A, NRSV

Aware of our great need for mercy and grace, both in our own lives and in the world around us, we hold before God all those areas where we long for Christ's transforming presence to bring healing and hope.

Wanting God is at the heart of all prayer and, whenever we pray, no matter how falteringly, our small flame of desire for God is met by God's infinite desire for us. Many passages in the words of Second Isaiah (the prophet who wrote chapters 40—55 during Israel's exile in Babylon in the sixth century BC) help us to understand how God longs to reach out to us. You may find it helpful to read slowly and prayerfully the verses printed below, and then to linger on any word or phrase that speaks to you in particular.

> *'Comfort, O comfort my people,' says your God. 'Speak tenderly to Jerusalem.'*
> ISAIAH 40:1–2

'You are my servant, I have chosen you and not cast you off; do not fear, for I am with you.'
ISAIAH 41:9–10

'Do not fear, for I have redeemed you; I have called you by name, you are mine... You are precious in my sight, and honoured, and I love you.'
ISAIAH 43:1, 4

Being still

Be silent, all people, before the Lord; for he has roused himself from his holy dwelling.
ZECHARIAH 2:13

Even if we can find only a few minutes, making space in the day when we can pause and be still and quiet can help to anchor us in God and keep us connected to the mystery of the incarnation that lies at the heart of this season.

In quiet prayer we become open and receptive to the God who gazes at us with eyes of love. Here we shed all our roles and images of ourselves. We do not have to do or achieve anything; we are simply present, giving our consent for Christ to come into our hearts and abide in us (John 15:4).

'The eternal birth must take place in you.'
MEISTER ECKHART, 1260–1327

For God alone my soul waits in silence; from him comes my salvation.
PSALM 62:1

In the silence I receive once more
this gift of my life from you, O God.
Hold me in your stillness,
simplify me,
and take possession of me.

The great 'O's of Advent

There is an ancient Christian practice of using a set of seven prayers expressing longing for Christ's coming, each starting with the word 'O', and taking one each evening from 17 to 23 December. This imaginative and slightly unusual custom is still observed in many cathedrals and churches today as part of the liturgical preparation for Christmas. These 'Advent Antiphons' are usually said or sung at the beginning and end of Mary's Song, the Magnificat, in the service of Evensong or Vespers. The imagery traditionally used in these prayers comes mostly from the Old Testament, and has been developed in a variety of ways. For example:

O Wisdom, breath of God, guide us and draw us closer to you.
O Lord of Israel, appearing to Moses in the burning bush and on Mount Sinai, come and save us.
O Root and Flower of Jesse's line, born into the house of David, all nations are silent in reverence before you.
O Key of David, free us from the prison of guilt and sin.
O Morning Star, radiance of the Father, shine on our darkness.
O King of the Nations, cornerstone holding us all together, strengthen us.
O Emmanuel, God with us—come!

You may like to use this basic outline, perhaps developing these themes in your own words. Or you could adapt the idea further by writing a different set, such as:

O Light of the World…
O Living Water…
O Bearer of Mercy…
O Lover and Friend…

or any other images that resonate for you.

Some people like to write out their 'O's for Advent using colour, calligraphy or drawings. Another possibility is to repeat your 'O's quietly to yourself or to sing them throughout the day. While there are numerous different ways of weaving the Advent 'O's into our prayer life, their purpose is always the same, to give voice to our fundamental human need for Christ's spirit to come and work in us and the world.

John the Baptist

A voice cries out, 'In the wilderness prepare the way of the Lord, make straight in the desert a highway for our God.'
ISAIAH 40:3

John the Baptist is a challenging figure, wild and ascetic, living alone in the desert and preaching a message of uncompromisingly high standards and rigorous judgment to all who have flocked to hear him (Luke 3:4–17). Yet there is another side to John. In his earlier life, he must have had an intimate, even homely, relationship with Jesus. They would almost certainly have played together as children in the Galilean countryside, since their mothers were first cousins and lived relatively close to each other (see Luke 1:39–56). And as they both grew into manhood, John must have begun to realise that there was something extraordinary about his cousin. So now he has obeyed God's call to go into the fierce wilderness of Judea, fasting, praying and telling his hearers to make themselves ready for the coming among them of Jesus, whose living and dying will change the world for ever.

John always points away from himself, embracing his identity as simply the messenger and insisting that he is not worthy even to untie Jesus' sandals (Luke 3:16). Once his task of proclamation is done, John announces, in a moment of supreme humility, 'He must increase, but I must decrease' (John 3:30). These words make a good watchword for any of us who, in our own context, are seeking to serve Christ and reflect his love in the world.

A ring of Advent candles

Making things with symbolic meaning can be as prayerful as using words. The basic concept of an Advent wreath or ring has developed in a variety of ways in different cultures, and we can participate in this delightful custom in whatever way works for us. If we do not have much time, we can simply place four red or white candles in a circle, each in its own holder and surrounded by some greenery. If we want to be more adventurous, we can fix the four candles to a round base or ring, surrounding them with evergreens (a symbolic reminder that the life of Jesus is eternal) and decorations such as ribbons, small fir cones and berries. A gold central candle can also be added, to be lit on Christmas Day.

The way we use our Advent wreath is also up to us. In most churches, the first candle is lit on Advent Sunday, and on the second Sunday the original candle is lit plus one other, and so on. But they can be lit at any time, especially if we have a ring of candles at home. Some people light them daily, perhaps at meals or at the beginning or end of each day.

As well as anticipating the coming of the light of Christ into the world, each candle carries its own meaning. One tradition in Germany (where the Advent wreath originated) sees the candles as standing for hope, peace, joy and love. They can also represent the forerunners of Jesus:

- First candle: the Patriarchs (Abraham, Isaac and Jacob)
- Second candle: the Old Testament prophets
- Third candle: John the Baptist
- Fourth candle: Mary, the mother of Jesus

Another possibility is to make each candle into a sign of commitment to a particular kind of prayer or action. You can choose your own themes, and the framework below is just one example:

- First candle: **a sign of thankfulness** for the love, light and beauty we encounter in our daily lives
- Second candle: **a sign of sorrow** for our sins and failings
- Third candle: **a sign of caring**, praying that we may be more alert to the opportunities for generosity and sharing that come our way
- Fourth candle: **a sign of trust** as we keep our gaze on Jesus in the midst of our activity and the turbulence of world events

You may like to write your own prayers to go with each candle, or you could simply light them in silence. Do whatever feels right for you.

Opening up to the light

Then the glory of the Lord shall be revealed.
ISAIAH 40:5

Besides this, you know what time it is, how it is now the moment for you to wake from sleep. For salvation is nearer to us now than when we became believers; the night is far gone, the day is near. Let us then lay aside the works of darkness and put on the armour of light.
ROMANS 13:11–12

Prayer in the dark does not need words, but presence, poise and a mixture of contentment and longing. Prayer before dawn, with no more than a candle and the curtains open, waiting for the light, likewise has no need of words, and no need of witnesses… a time when, simply, the heart will muse in silence on Christ and his coming.
SISTER ROSEMARY, SLG, IN *FAIRACRES CHRONICLE* WINTER 2005, VOLUME 38, NO. 2, P. 1

As the watchman waits for the dawn,
so do I wait for you, O Christ my saviour.

The light of each new day
after the long, dark night
is a reminder of your coming, O Christ.

Thank you that your unquenchable light
has overcome all our darkness.
Help me to recognise your light and presence
within the world around me,
and grant me the grace to live each day
as you would wish.

I open up to you any areas that especially need your love and mercy:
in my own life…
in the lives of people I know…
in the wider world…
Come, O Christ our Light, and illumine our darkness.
Kindle in our hearts the fire of your love.

Ready and watchful

Matthew 25:1–13

Unlike at most weddings in the West today, it was the bride who had to wait for the bridegroom at the start of Middle Eastern weddings in the time of Jesus. Attended by her maidens and decked in fine robes, the bride would wait while the bridegroom engaged in preliminary celebrations and then proceeded with his men friends to collect her. As soon as the bride's attendants heard him coming, they would go out to meet him. Then a torch-lit procession would escort the bride and groom to his ancestral home, and this part of the proceedings could take a long time, as friends would line the route and sweetmeats were given out on the way. So the servants at a wedding banquet would have a significant wait before welcoming the bridegroom with his bride. What better image for our own preparation for the celebration of Jesus' coming? The challenge to be ready to receive Jesus into our lives applies at any time, but Advent focuses our attention in a particular way on the need to be constantly watchful and alert to Jesus' presence among us and to the promptings of his Spirit.

You might also like to read a variation on this theme in Jesus' parable in Luke 12:35–38. Here we see a group of servants faithfully staying awake as they wait for their master who, this time, has been a guest at a wedding feast. To their surprise, their vigilance is rewarded by the master's serving them at table when he returns, rather than the other way round.

In both these stories the themes of *lit lamps* and *keeping awake* represent a quality of expectancy and readiness that we need to adopt. We are not expected to be perfect in order to receive Christ, but we do need to acknowledge how much we need the mercy, love and grace that he is waiting to pour into us as soon as we open up to him. One of the most important things in the Christian life is keeping the door of our heart open. Once we do this we may be surprised, like the servants in the parable, by the outrageous generosity of the Saviour who comes not to be served but to serve and to give his life for love of us all.

Arms outstretched

Some hermits in the Egyptian desert in the fourth and fifth centuries, and certain ascetic monks in sixth-century Ireland, made it part of their regular devotions to stand facing east through the whole of each Saturday night, waiting for the dawn that signified Christ's resurrection. They stood with their arms outstretched. Most of us probably do not have the stamina to perform such a dramatic feat of endurance, but we can still learn from these eccentric and saintly characters about the value of using our bodies in prayer. Sometimes it is easier to express our deepest longings before God with a physical gesture than with words, and the custom of standing to pray goes back to Old Testament times, when people regularly stood before the Lord with their arms outstretched toward heaven (for example, 1 Kings 8:54, Psalm 141:2). A painting on the wall of the third-century catacomb of St Priscilla in Rome shows a woman praying with her arms out wide, in what has traditionally become known as the *orans* (Latin for 'praying') position. We still see this practice today in various parts of the church, such as when a priest stands at the altar of the Eucharist with arms outstretched or when worshippers raise their arms to God during praise songs.

For us in Advent, this gesture of stretching out our arms may help us to open ourselves up to Christ at a deep level. We do not necessarily have to stand. When we are sitting down, simply lifting up the palms of our hands while keeping our elbows bent is a good way to invite Christ into our lives and into the world around us.

Come, Lord Jesus

One of the earliest known Christian prayers is the phrase found in Paul's first letter to the Corinthians: *Marana tha*, which means 'Our Lord, come!' in Aramaic, the everyday language spoken by Jesus and his disciples (1 Corinthians 16:22). Many people today use these four syllables *Ma-ra-na-tha* to help them become still and inwardly quiet before God, repeating them silently in what is known as Christian meditation (although any word or phrase can be used). Another way of using this most ancient of prayers, either in its original form or in the more common translation, 'Come, Lord Jesus', is to weave it into a simple liturgy. Here is an example:

Marana tha: Come, Lord Jesus,
speak to my fears,
guide me when I am confused
and help me to put my trust in you.

Marana tha: Come, Lord Jesus,
speak to my hurts,
stay with me as I struggle to forgive
and help me to rely on you.

Marana tha: Come, Lord Jesus,
speak to my longings,
show me where love and truth are found
and help me to recognise your promptings in my life.

Marana tha: Come, Lord Jesus,
where hearts are broken and lives ruined by violence, hatred and war;
where there is no food or water and the rich world cares too little;
show me how best to serve others,
that I may make your loving presence known in the world.
Marana tha: Come, Lord Jesus.
Amen

Judgment and mercy

For centuries, Christians have taken Advent as a time to ponder four themes that might at first seem alarming: death, judgment, heaven and hell. Yet these subjects are not designed to frighten us into goodness or belief, but are there to remind us that our behaviour and attitudes do matter and that the light of Christ throws into sharp relief our inner lives and outward behaviour. In the end there is no hiding from the truth about ourselves, and we are asked to pause and examine the values, motives and desires that underlie the ways in which we think and act, so that we can then experience the divine mercy, which is freely given once we turn to receive it.

Sometimes 'judgment' is confused with 'punishment' or even 'vengeance', but they are not the same. In the end, as St John of the Cross puts it, we shall be judged by love. We do need to be rigorously honest with ourselves, and yet it is because God's infinite love and compassion come to meet us that we can have the confidence to open up the whole of our lives and not just the respectable and 'worthy' parts. The very point at which we feel most fragmented, lost and ashamed is the point where Jesus is pressing most keenly to love, heal and remake us. We see this time and again in the Gospels, especially in the way Jesus responds to those whose lives are broken or a mess. And we can be encouraged by Jesus' parable of the tax collector who comes to the temple with no agenda other than to seek forgiveness for his many sins and goes home at peace with himself and with God (Luke 18:9–14).

Jesus came not to condemn us but to free us from all that stops us being our best and truest selves. Healthy self-examination steers us between the two extremes of a casual and careless approach to sin on the one hand, and excessive guilt on the other. Facing the truth about ourselves may be uncomfortable, but in the end it sets us on a path towards wholeness, healing and peace.

A travelling companion

One way of praying when life is full of activity—and Advent is often a busy time—is to take a word or phrase that resonates with you from scripture, from a hymn or prayer or from some other source, and to repeat it gently to yourself at odd moments through the day. Words used in this way can become a good travelling companion, helping us to reconnect with God at any moment and in any situation, no matter how hectic or trying.

You might like to take a verse or sentence that has spoken to you in this issue of *Quiet Spaces*, or there may be a favourite word or phrase that you have used before. Thinking and breathing the name of 'Jesus' takes a lot of beating, especially during Advent.

Advent (2)

Janet Fletcher

The Annunciation

Luke 1:26–38

As we begin the last two weeks of Advent, let us turn to Mary and Joseph, the angel's visit and the unfolding story and mystery that draw us ever closer to the incarnation.

Gabriel's visitation to Mary will no doubt be familiar. It may raise a number of questions within as we seek to understand what took place or imagine how we would react if we were Mary. What were Mary's thoughts as Gabriel brought her the news that she had been chosen to bring to birth the Son of God? The Gospel account doesn't tell us how much time they spent in conversation and how long it was before Mary gave her answer. It seems, though, to have been a short meeting!

When I sensed myself being called to ordained ministry, it took me a long time before I felt able to give an answer to God, and when I did it was a very hesitant 'yes'. There may have been an occasion in your own life when it has taken time to discern an answer to a call or problem. Yet Mary replies 'yes', with an underlying sense of calmness, to Gabriel, to God.

Did Mary understand what was being asked of her? Like Mary, we too have the choice to walk with God, to enter into that pilgrim journey, which begins and continues every time we say 'yes'. We return to Mary's 'yes' a little further on in these weeks.

Pilgrimage through Advent

Let us reflect on how our pilgrimage through Advent is to continue, depending upon the constraints on our time and the commitments and responsibilities that we have.

The question to ask as we draw closer to Christmas, and as the busyness of this time tries to overtake us, is: what is Advent? It may seem strange to reflect on this now, as we are halfway through Advent, yet it may be that this is the right time. What would be your ideal Advent?

What is Advent?

A long-ago call lost amidst the noise of a material world?
A forgotten dream and story discarded on the journey from childhood to adulthood?
A hope too painful to consider in the midst of loneliness, death and economic collapse?

What is Advent?

God's Word silenced by shopping lists, baking trays, tinsel and wrapping paper?
God's Word ignored in busy preparation for parties, meals and family get-togethers?
God's Word limited to a picture on a Christmas card, and the annual Lessons and Carols?

What is Advent?

Love stretching out from heaven to earth, all-encompassing in joy and excitement?
Love with passion, all-enfolding, all-encircling, all-welcoming?

Love poured out to sustain, drawing to itself, all who are faithful, questioning, uncertain?
Love coming in the Word made flesh?
Love that is hope?

Known, called and chosen

Place yourself and your name within the liturgy, and in prayer ponder what it may be that God is asking of you, or the way in which you feel you may be called to serve God.

I, God, know your name..., and by name I call you to follow me:
Help me to follow you.

I have created you... in my own image:
Help me to see that and rejoice in it.

I call you... as I called Mary, to become the person you can be:
Help me to become that person.

I have chosen you in love..., and speak into your heart:
Open my ears and my heart to your presence, to your voice speaking in and above the tumult of my life.

I called and chose you..., and call you by your own name:
You, O God, know me better than I know myself, and still you have called and chosen me to follow and serve you. Help me to answer your call in truth, and in honesty, and in faith.

I call you...

What is your response and answer? What do you feel and believe God is calling you to? This could be a major change in life or something small—one is as valid as the other.

Finding silence in Advent

To find silence at any time of the year can be difficult, and during Advent it may feel that wherever we go, we are surrounded by noise, music and the sounds of Christmas. Yet, if we seek some quiet time with God, then we will find it. An oasis of stillness, in which we can discover a much needed inner peace. To find a space for silence and silent prayer in this Advent season can bring to us both renewal and refreshment for the days ahead.

Set aside a time when you know you will not be disturbed.

Sit in a place that is comfortable. It may be helpful to light a candle or to play some relaxing music in the background.

Ask God to be with you in this time of quietness and stillness. If there is anything that you particularly seek in prayer and life at this moment, then bring it to God.

Seek to rest very simply and quietly with God.

If thoughts and words come to you, then bring these to God too.

Spend as much time as feels right in this silent prayer.

At the end of the prayer, give thanks to God, and ask God to be with you in these remaining days of Advent.

Mince pies and wrapping paper

What do mince pies and Christmas wrapping paper 'say' or mean to you? Both have been on sale in the shops for a number of months, and you may not want to see either until next Christmas! Yet, they are both a part of this season of Advent, and they bring to us the quickly-passing days—maybe, too, the reminder of presents still to be wrapped.

I enjoy baking, but have never mastered the art of making pastry, so I always buy my mince pies. I'm not too good, either, at wrapping presents to look like a creative piece of artwork. Like me, you may find lots of bits of wrapping paper, coloured string or ribbon left over, and, for bakers, bits of pastry that has been rolled out once too often to hold its filling of mincemeat.

These leftovers could have a use. Here is a creative way of praying on your own, with other family members or with children; as a way to find a little stillness now, or after Christmas, when Christmas cards can be used as well.

Pastry: can be rolled out and twisted into a variety of shapes. It can be coloured with food colouring, and other ingredients can be added, and personalised perhaps for each person in the family. Offer a prayer for that person as the pastry is given shape. Sometimes, simply to 'play' with the pastry as you would with a piece of clay can be surprisingly calming and evoke a quiet prayer or release inner tensions.

Paper: have a large sheet of paper, a glue stick and a pen near you as you wrap your presents. With the leftover bits of paper, be as creative as you like to bring together a pattern or collage. As you glue the bits of wrapping paper into place, hold the person who will receive that present in your heart along with the gift they will discover on opening. You may wish to write their names down as well. If you have cooked the leftover pastry into shapes, this too can form part of the collage.

The collage becomes a reminder of those who have shared this season with you. Maybe those to whom you offer hospitality could write their names on the sheet. As they do this, if you can, ask them to offer a prayer for you.

Hospitality: Mary visits Elizabeth

Luke 1:39–45

The offering of hospitality is part of our call as Christians but also plays a very important part in the coming season of Christmas. Many of you will be offering the hospitality of your home and yourself to family, which can cause a certain amount of stress as we seek to fit as much as we can into such a short space of time! Yet, to welcome family and friends at this time can also bring support, help and companionship— a time to relax, share and laugh.

Mary must have felt sure of her welcome by Zechariah and Elizabeth, and that they would offer the hospitality she needed. As Elizabeth welcomed Mary, so her unborn son welcomed the unborn Son Mary carried.

Meeting unexpectedly, with words of joy spoken,
those cradled in the safe warmth of each one's womb
leapt in joyful recognition.
Each stretching out, unfolding their growing limbs
until their appointed time to seek in birth
the hospitality of God they are called to bring to a welcoming
unwelcoming world.

Now, revealed Son to son unborn,
in divine recognition and power reaching
into the depths of their hidden places swaddled in love,
touched with love, a love that passes all understanding,

a love which communicates, speaks heart to heart,
revealing the hospitality of God indwelling,
bringing to birth all that is to be, and will be for each,
Son and son.

Who will you be offering hospitality to during the coming weeks?

How will you offer 'hospitality' to God—making space in the busyness for conversation and companionship with him in the quietness and depth of your being?

To wait patiently

In the Psalms we read: 'Be still before the Lord and wait patiently for him' (Psalm 37:7, NRSV). At this time in Advent, how easy is it to 'be still' with God, and to be patient with ourselves as we seek space for prayer?

In a time of quiet, read through the words of this prayer and the questions that follow. How patient are we, in these weeks of Advent, as the days speed by, bringing us ever closer to the joy and the celebrations of Christmas Day?

How patient you are in your love,
Creator and Nurturer of all that is seen and unseen.
Watching as each blade of grass struggles through the soil,
each trickling brook finds its pathway to the sea.
How patient you are with those you call by name,
and visit, bringing startling news.
Watching as they, and we, seek to make sense of your presence in our lives,
in my own seeking to understand all you call to birth from deep within me.
How patient you are in your love,

Creator and Nurturer of us, who you call 'my children',
of me, who you call 'my child'.
You watch with infinite patience as I struggle to find my own way
in life,
and are with me in patient guidance.
You seek out the beauty and the potential within me,
as you did with Mary,
to draw from me all that I am, and all that I can be.
Be with me in patient waiting,
that I may know it too.

How patient a person are you, and how has that changed, if it has, in the build-up to Christmas Day?

At this Advent time, where and how do you 'wait upon God' in prayer, and in life?

What is the prayer you seek to offer to God? Which areas of your life at this moment are in need of the grace of patience?

Magnificat

Luke 1:46–56

Mary's song of praise, the Magnificat, finds itself placed within the Anglican heritage of Evening Prayer. Likewise, the prophecy spoken by Zechariah, the Benedictus (Luke 1:68–79) spoken after the naming of John the Baptist, has also become a part of the daily office at Morning Prayer.

The words of Mary reveal a powerful proclamation of faith and belief in all that God will do and can do. It brings to us a fuller image of Mary than the quiet, saintly one sometimes portrayed through carols. This is Mary's personal song to God, her prayer of faith. It can become a prayer for all of us.

As we seek to follow the way of God, and say our 'yes' to God, then we too could—should—echo these words of Mary.

Take some time to read through the passage.

Which phrases or words seem particularly important to you?

Who is the God who is revealed to you in these words of Mary?

Then think about and try to write your own Magnificat, your own song of praise to God. What would you include? What words of praise? What would be the intercession? Words that express your own understanding of God, the needs of the world in which we live, words giving thanks to God, and words that remember the necessity of intercession for peace, justice and equality.

Yes!

Mary says, 'Yes.' A simple word of affirmation, of agreement. It says, 'I will, I will do what you ask.' A simple word that holds within it strength, determination and power. This 'yes' spoken by Mary brings new life into being. A new life that will change the whole world— change you and me.

Yes. A word that is easy to say on the surface of our lives, but how easy to say when taken from the deepest place within us—a place where we meet with God and are met by God?

Our own 'yes' is not one but many. One spoken daily, spoken often on our pilgrim's path of faith.

Yes?

O God, I make and give
my 'yes' to you this day.
A 'yes' that embraces
the whole of me, my faith, my life,
my limitations, my doubts,
my certainties, my struggling to understand.

I offer my 'yes' today,
again,
for the first time,
knowing that you are with me.
In my saying 'yes' to you,
your love, your Spirit and presence within,
empower me through that love
to reveal you to the world,
bring to birth from within me
all that you call me to be,
know I can be.

Help me not to hesitate
in my saying 'yes'.
May my 'yes' say and mean
'I will, I will do what you ask.'
May my 'yes' echo the 'yes' of Mary,
in faith and in truth.

May my 'yes' guide me ever closer to you,
O God, Emmanuel, God with me,
now and for always.
Amen

The road to Bethlehem

The road to Bethlehem began long before Mary and Joseph made the journey to be registered for the census. Both Mary and Joseph had been visited by the angel Gabriel, which meant journeying within themselves to realise the truth of the words spoken to them, and to find acceptance of all they were called to do and give to God. The visit of the angel to Joseph may not have been quite as dramatic as the visit to Mary, but it was transforming nonetheless.

How difficult was that inner spiritual journey to hear, and meet with, the voice and call of God? Who helped and supported them? What part did friends and family play at this challenging and perhaps frightening time? From that moment on, they share not only their lives together, but also the calling from God to care for the son who is to come and is to be a part of their family.

Many people would have touched the lives of Mary and Joseph as they waited for the birth of the Christ-child. What effect did Mary and Joseph have on those they met and knew? Soon they would travel that road to Bethlehem and bring to the world the fulfilment of God's promise to Mary. The birth of God's Son is a birth that would be the very beginning of a much longer pilgrim path to be travelled; by them and by us.

When we look at our lives, the inward spiritual journey and the outer physical journeys we make each day, then many people, too, will have been influential in shaping the person we are today. They may not be aware of all they have given to us, as we may never know the depth or extent of how we have touched the lives of those we have met over the course of our life.

In a time of quietness, reflect upon the people who have been a part of your own journey, your own 'road to Bethlehem', following your own call to faith. On a large piece of paper, draw a figure or write your name in the centre. Around this, draw or write the names of those who have shaped your life or influenced you in any way. These may be people alive today or those who have died, people you know well or have known only briefly. It may be someone you have never met, but you have heard them speak, read something they have written or heard a line in a song they have sung.

Give thanks to God for them, and the many more, unknown perhaps at this moment, who will be a part of your ongoing pilgrimage journey; your own road to Bethlehem and beyond.

Creating and recreating God

'You show me the path of life. In your presence there is fullness of joy; in your right hand are pleasures forevermore.'
PSALM 16:11

Come, Lord Jesus: Maranatha.
Creating and re-creating God:
The world has moved through the seasons drawing us once more to Advent.
My soul thirsts for God, for the living God.
The people walking in darkness will see the light, the light of peace, righteousness and justice.
My soul thirsts for the Light of God, the Light of the living God.
A shoot, coming out from the stump of Jesse, shall shoot forth branches of wisdom, understanding and knowledge.
My soul thirsts for the Wisdom of God, the Wisdom of the living God.
The wolf and the lamb, the cow and the bear shall be as one in love, a love of acceptance you call the world to desire.
My soul thirsts for the true Love of God, the true Love of the living God.
In calling into being your Word, you speak into the world and into the hearts of all with ears to hear you.
My soul thirsts for the Word of God, the Word of the living God.

A time for silent prayer:

'Let the words of my mouth and the meditation of my heart be acceptable to you, O Lord, my rock and my redeemer.'
PSALM 19:14

Come, Lord Jesus: Maranatha.

The star is coming

Advent is coming to a close, and the celebrations of Christmas and the birth of the Christ-child will soon be upon us.

Star in the night sky,
swirling, struggling
into brightness of being
to fulfil its prophesied role,
to light the way for
all creation to see
God's world transformed,
touched by God,
God coming soon to birth.

Star in the night sky,
starting its ascension
to its appointed place,
a sign, a signal, a symbol
to all of a new birth,
a new beginning for all
as love in all of its
Beauty and Truth
will soon come to birth.

Take some time to reflect upon these weeks of Advent, the busy days and the quiet moments. Ponder your feelings and emotions—stress, joy, peace, anxiety, love, thanksgiving, doubt—and when and where you felt them. What are your feelings and emotions at this moment? Offer them all to God and ask for God's peace, a peace that passes all understanding, to be with you now and in the days ahead.

During these Advent weeks a pilgrim journey has taken place, a journey that leads us along the road to Bethlehem. How has the pilgrim path you have travelled through these weeks helped you to ensure times of quiet prayer?

How has the pilgrim path you have travelled through Advent helped you to prepare for the coming celebrations and the birth of the Son of God?

Are you ready to enter, with a deepening faith and sense of God with you, the days now coming?

The Christmas seasons

Sally Smith

Introduction

After Advent, the season of waiting and preparing, we move to the celebratory seasons of Christmas, Epiphany and New Year. Advent has been a time of preparing. Now here it is, Christmas, and all it brings—happy, sad, of God and secular, as the Christ-child is born in the stable with the animals, the shepherds and the kings, and we give and receive presents, eat, visit…

It is good to pause in the midst of this to reflect on what is happening beneath the images we are given on our cards and in the media, to re-read the biblical story and remember what happened. This is a season of balance and compromise as we hold together the celebration of 'O come all ye faithful' with the stillness of 'Silent night'. Try to find some quiet places and times to spend with God over these couple of weeks.

If you feel as if there is too much quiet and space for reflection this Christmas, use some of it to enter the stillness of God on earth and join Mary in pondering the mystery and majesty of the events as we read them in the Bible.

This can be a good time to read the biblical story of the birth of Jesus: Luke 1:1—2:20. It can be helpful to use a different version from your usual one to gain a fresh perspective on the well-known story.

The Christmas tree

I have always found that there is something very special about the decorations on the tree. As a child, I looked forward to unwrapping them again and seeing which became old friends over the years, and I would spend hours looking at them, remembering stories about them from the past.

A few years ago I read an article that gave meanings to some of the different things we hang on our Christmas trees. It sounded somewhat twee and forced as I read it, but for some reason, as I decorated the tree that year I remembered some of what I had read, and I prayed through decorating the tree, remembering the meaning of different items as I hung them on the branches. While the tree remained in the house I was gently reminded of why those things were there, and God became present in the tinsel and glitter.

You could turn decorating the tree into a time of prayer, or, if the tree is already decorated, spend some time looking at it and what is hanging on it, and make the decorations your way in to prayer.

The tree itself is evergreen, representing the eternal life of Christ. Similarly, holly is evergreen but also has the blood-red berries and the thorns from Jesus' crown of thorns.

The lights are a reminder of Jesus as the light of the world; coloured lights are a reminder of the different people and nations of the world. Candles are a thank you to God for sending his Son and a reminder to shine as a light in the world.

The red ornaments echo Christ's shedding his blood and point towards his death and resurrection.

The stars are for the wise men, for their gifts, their determination to find Jesus, and their adoration of the baby Jesus.

The gold (tinsel, baubles, and so on) give a regal air for the King of kings.

Anything round (wreaths, baubles, and so on) has the sense of eternity, the never-ending circle and God's everlasting love for you and for others around the tree.

There are a couple of bells on my tree that ring out for the lost sheep—those I know, and those I don't know.

Of course, the angel sits on top of the tree, overlooking all and announcing the good news, singing, 'Glory to God in the highest heaven, and on earth peace among those whom he favours!' (Luke 2:14).

And Santa sits beneath the tree because God wants us to be happy and have fun and give and receive presents with people we love.

Mary

Mary is central to the birth of Jesus, pictured on our cards holding Jesus or looking at him lying in the manger. We are also told that she treasured and pondered the words of the shepherds after their visit (Luke 2:19). We hear the story each year and can become over-familiar with the events, losing sight of what is really happening to Mary. It would not have been plain sailing from conception onwards. She would have been shamed in her community. Becoming pregnant while betrothed was sufficient grounds for stoning at that time. Apart from Elizabeth, she would have had few friends. After all the proclamations of the angel, reality hit and she found herself in poor conditions, expecting a baby she had been told would be holy and would be called the Son of the Most High. Through it all, she shows humility, faith and obedience. She remains true to what she has been told despite the difficulties she experiences.

Take the account of the Christmas story from Luke (1:26—2:20). We read here of what happened to Mary in those nine months from the visit of the angel to the visit of the shepherds. It can seem as if we know very little of what happened, but read it carefully and note what Mary is told—what she knows about her baby. You might like to write it out, seeing in black and white what she was told, what she was trying to understand. We read it with hindsight, but Mary didn't have that benefit.

Imagine hearing those words for the first time and beginning to take them in.

And then join Mary in pondering these things, holding them in the silence as she did and allowing the words to enter your heart. Maybe end by returning to Mary's song of praise (Luke 1:46–55) and making it your prayer.

Glory to God

Christmas is a time of mixed emotions and responses. We love to see family and friends, but it can be exhausting, and in the midst of winter it's also nice to snuggle down for a quiet evening with a book or a film. There are big Christmas parties and quieter moments, huge carol services and the quiet anticipation that comes with Advent. The shepherds too had their loud and quiet moments. The story of the shepherds in Luke 2:8–20 begins with the host of angels and ends with the shepherds glorifying and praising God, but in between is the time in the stable, which both Mary and the shepherds treasure and ponder.

In the Old Testament, the 'heavenly host' is used interchangeably for stars and other celestial bodies, and for angels. So it is fitting here to have the shepherds out under the sky and the stars and greeted by an army of angels. The praise of God they experienced here would have travelled with them to see the baby and emerged afterwards in their praise for all they had heard and seen.

Join the shepherds and the angelic host in praise for all God has done. Several popular carols do this well:

'All glory be to God on high, and to the earth be peace'

'Glory to God in the highest'

'Hark! the herald angels sing'

Spend some time with these or other words known to you, and praise God for his gift of his Son to the world.

Nativity scene

Take a careful look at cards you may have that portray the shepherds visiting Jesus in the stable. Then read Luke 2:15–20.

On Christmas cards the shepherds around the manger, if they are revealing any emotion at all, often show a mixture of surprise, love and awe. They tend to be fairly clean and well mannered, and look as if they have just popped in briefly. Mary always seems to be taking their visit in her stride, as if it is normal for every young girl with a baby in a stable to have a crowd of shepherds descend on her.

I like the experience of a shepherd in Michael Morpurgo's story *On Angel's Wings* (Egmont Books, 2006). As a young boy, he was the first visitor at the stable, and Mary invited him to hold Jesus. He describes those precious moments and how they, and the child he held, have stayed with him into his old age. He doesn't tell the other shepherds about this, knowing that they won't believe him and will make fun of him, but he shares it with his grandchildren.

What would it be like to visit the baby Jesus in the manger and to be invited to hold him?

Join the shepherds as they journey down from the fields to Bethlehem. Notice the moon and the stars and the stillness of the night. Feel the fresh night air. Look at the stars in the dark sky. Listen to the quietness around as you travel through the fields and then into the town. Listen to the other shepherds as they take in what has happened and what they are doing. How do they make sense of it all?

Stand with the shepherds outside the stable as they decide if they are in the right place and who will go in first. Peep with them through the crack in the old wooden doors.

Enter with them and take in the scene. Notice Mary and Joseph. See the place where Jesus is laid. Watch as the shepherds gather round. Listen as they describe their adventures and leave their gifts.

Mary gives the baby to one of the shepherds to hold. Jesus is then passed between the shepherds. Watch them as they each have their precious moment. Then one of the shepherds passes Jesus to you. You hold him in your arms. What are you thinking? Hold the tension of this being a baby and being Jesus, God's Son. When the time comes, pass him on.

Leave with the shepherds and spend a few moments outside reflecting on what has been happening in the stable and how you feel about it.

Nativity

Find a Christmas card with a nativity scene on it, and look at how Jesus has been portrayed in the picture. Usually he is shown either bathed in light or with light coming from him.

> *He is portrayed bathed in light, quietly lying.*
> *Yet he is only a baby.*
> *The onlookers are lit with his light and look on in awe and*
> *astonishment.*
> *Yet he is only a baby.*
> *Mary looks on quietly, lovingly.*
> *Yet he is only a baby.*

But he is not only a baby. He is also God, divine, the Son of God.

The artist is trying to express what we struggle to grasp; that this baby is a baby and yet is also God. We cannot get the two thoughts to go together, and artists try to do this by the use of light and by the expressions of those watching. The light showing the otherness of this particular baby, the expressions and actions of the onlookers showing the recognition that this is not just any baby.

How else might this be represented? It might not make a good Christmas card, but how would you represent God coming to earth as a baby? What sights, sounds, touch sensations would you use to express this?

Stay with these sensations as you meet the baby who is God.

A child has been born—for us!

Isaiah 9:2–7

This is the first of the messianic prophecies in Isaiah, telling of the coming Messiah. It is in the form of a hymn or psalm and is often compared with Psalm 2. It tells of a child being born to *us*. This is God getting involved, being prepared to get his hands dirty, and it resonates with our desire for the humble and authentic, especially in the 21st century when so much of what we see in the media portrays a false, manufactured image.

THE MESSAGE version of the Bible uses, 'A child has been born—for Us!' as the heading for this chapter, emphasising that the child is for *us*; for us as individuals, for us as church communities, and for the whole planet. The passage can be read as being for each of those audiences.

Take this passage and read it slowly. If you know it well, it might help to read a different translation or version of the Bible to bring a fresh viewpoint.

Read it again, this time being open to phrases or words that speak to you. Pause at a phrase, repeating it in your head and allowing it to travel deeper inside you. Don't try to analyse the phrase, but receive it as a gift from God… accept it… cherish it… allow God to reveal its full significance for you.

Give each phrase time and space to unfold, but when you are ready, pause and then move on, ready for another phrase to be revealed.

You might like to write out the most important phrases and put them where you can be reminded of them, or write them in your journal if you use one.

Finish by thanking God for his gifts to you, for his gift of his Son for you.

New Year

St Ignatius recommends a daily Examen of Consciousness in which we look back over the past 24 hours and recognise where God has been present and where we have fallen short. It can be useful to do something similar at the end of the year, to recognise where God has been present in the past year and be conscious of his gifts to us, and to acknowledge our failings and hand them to God.

New Year often seems to intrude on the Christmas season, adding another dimension and distracting us from the birth of Christ. But the fact that it falls in the holiday period can give us the space to mark it and to reflect on the year that is past and the year to come.

Find a comfortable place to sit and maybe light a candle to bring God's revealing light into this time and into the past and future years. Pause and allow the busyness around you and the activity of the past few days to settle. Place yourself in God's unconditional love; whatever has happened this year, God loves you and will continue to love you.

Invite God to be present as you reflect on the past year.

Begin by asking the question: when has God been present to me this year?

Recognise those times when you have been particularly aware of God with you during the year, times when you have known his goodness and generosity. You will have been aware of some of these at the time, while for other encounters you will be recognising God's involvement for the first time.

Some people find it helpful to draw or write these as a way of focusing on what God has been doing.

Thank God for all he has been doing, for the things you have recognised, and those that still go unrecognised. Offer him your thanks and praise for what he has done and who he is.

Stay with this until you are ready to move on. When you are ready, begin to recognise the points in the past year when it has felt as if God were absent, the times when you have ignored or shunned him, the low points in the year. Don't dwell on guilt or fault, but recognise those places and times and invite God into them, allowing him to fill them with his love and then to take them and make them his. Remember, God loves us unconditionally; he loves us in our failings as well as our successes. Receive his forgiveness and his love.

Then turn to the blank page that is the coming year. What would you like to be written on that page? Ask God for your heart's desire.

What do you know will be on those pages? Hold these things before God, giving them to him, that he may be in them before you get there. If you have your new diary, you might like to offer that to God as a symbol of the coming year, giving him all it already holds and all it will hold.

'I said to the man who stood at the gate of the year, "Give me a light that I may tread safely into the unknown." And he replied, "Go out into the darkness and put your hand into the hand of God. That shall be to you better than light and safer than a known way!" So I went forth, and finding the hand of God, trod gladly into the night.'

MINNIE LOUISE HASKINS (1875–1957)

The visitors from the east

We know very little about these visitors. They are traditionally called kings because of references such as Isaiah 60:3, which suggests that kings will visit the Son of God soon after his birth, and Psalm 72:10–11, in which kings fall down and worship and bring gifts to the coming king.

We do not know how many visitors there were. Because they brought three gifts, we traditionally assume that there were three. We do, however, know what gifts they brought with them—gold, frankincense and myrrh.

These gifts were rare and precious: the visitors were giving the best that they could manage. They gave anonymously; we don't even know their names (although tradition has given them names).

Alongside the giving of the gifts, they worshipped the child. This was not a separate act, but combined with the giving of gifts. Whatever their status, they recognised Jesus as greater than they were, someone before whom the only possible action was to kneel down and worship.

The gifts tell us about the givers and about their perception of the one receiving the gifts. With hindsight, we can see a symbolism behind the gifts: gold for a king, frankincense representing deity or priesthood, and myrrh for suffering and death, or, as the last verse of 'We three kings of Orient are' (John Henry Hopkins, 1857), puts it: 'Glorious now behold him arise, King and God and sacrifice.'

But did the visitors know the full meaning behind their three gifts?

Some of the gifts you have received this Christmas will have told you about the person giving them. Some gifts will tell you of the giver's perception of you, and others of their insight into who you are.

But what of the gifts God gives us? What do they tell us of God, the giver? What do they tell of who he believes us to be and wants us to become?

Spend some time acknowledging the gifts God has given you in the past year, and recognising the giver behind those gifts. What do you learn of God from this?

What do you learn of his view of you from his gifts?

What do you learn of his longings for you and your life?

Stay before the generous giver and thank him for his gifts. You might like to write a prayer or letter of thanks.

Gold

Gold is a gift for a king. Kings wear golden crowns and have gold trim on their robes. So gold is an appropriate gift for the King of kings. Gold was also an important feature of the tabernacle. The ark of the covenant was covered by a slab of gold, and standing beside it was the incense altar, which was overlaid with gold. The temple Solomon built was similarly decorated with much gold—a material suitable for a king and suitable for God.

But what do we know about gold?

It is dug from the earth.

It is refined in fire to make it pure.

It is beautiful, both in the small amounts most of us are likely to encounter and when used on buildings, statues, and so on, when it catches the light and shines so amazingly.

It can endure fire. It loses nothing in fire—it keeps the same weight, colour and nature.

It is easily shaped.

It can be strengthened by creating an alloy with another metal.

Find something gold or golden. Hold it and feel it. Feel the weight and the softness, the warmth and the hard edges. Hold it with love.

Feel how it has become smooth over the years as it has been worn. See the scratches and dents in it and the character they bring. See how it has moulded to the wearer. See the hallmark that tells of its quality and background.

Look at it. See the way it reflects the light. Can you see something of yourself reflected in it?

Then turn to God and allow him to see you in the way you have seen the gold.

Allow him to hold you, to feel the warmth and the hard edges, to hold you with love.

Acknowledge before God how your edges have been smoothed over the years and how you have been dented and scratched, and allow God to love those scratches and dents.

Recognise how you have been worn and moulded to God. See his mark on you: you are his, and he has claimed you with his mark.

Ask God how you reflect his light as he holds you. Ask that you may reflect his beauty and love into the world.

Allow yourself to be presented to Jesus with the other three gifts, and allow him to take you and hold you.

Frankincense

In the Bible, frankincense is used when making an offering to God. It becomes a symbol of God's name (Malachi 1:11) and an emblem of prayer (Psalm 141:2). It is sweet-smelling and so is assumed to be pleasing to God. It was given to Jesus as a symbol of his priesthood, his deity and his life of prayer.

In the holy temple there were two altars. One was made of bronze, and was used for sacrifices; the other was made of gold, and was the altar of incense that stood before the veil at the entrance to the Holy of Holies. Every morning and evening incense would be burnt on the altar of incense, creating a regular offering of prayer to God. Twice a day the incense rose through the temple, symbolising the rising of prayers to God. In Psalm 141:2 David asks that his prayer be counted as incense before God, and in Revelation 8 the prayers of the people are combined with the incense being offered on the altar as they rise to God.

Altars are for sacrifices, and our prayer can be a sacrifice—of time, energy and love. Frankincense comes from the brokenness of the tree as it is cut to allow the resin to seep out and be collected as tears of frankincense.

At this time of year we often have scented candles around the house. Take one of these candles (or some incense if you have some) and smell it unlit.

Light the candle and watch the flame grow and shrink. As the flame dances or stills, see it point upwards.

Allow your thanks for this season and all it means to you to join the flame dancing towards God.

Allow your thoughts to wander to those in need and to be carried up with the flame and the scent towards God.

Notice the smell from the candle.

Allow your love for God to be drawn up with the prayers and allow his love for you to be drawn into you with the fragrance of the candle.

Read Psalm 141:2 or Song of Songs 1:2–3.

When you are ready, blow out the candle and allow the scent to linger as God's presence lingers with you.

Myrrh

Frankincense is sweet-smelling, but myrrh is bitter—as the song 'We three kings of Orient are' says, 'Myrrh is mine, its bitter perfume breathes a life of gathering gloom: sorrowing, sighing, bleeding, dying, sealed in the stone-cold tomb.'

Myrrh was used as incense, but was also used in embalming and so would have been one of the herbs and spices used by the women at the tomb. It was also mixed with wine and offered to Jesus on the cross. Myrrh very much points towards the cross, and so we are reminded with the gift of myrrh that the birth of Jesus is the first step towards the cross.

Myrrh was also included in the oils used for anointing. The oil used in 1 Samuel 16:13 to anoint David as king would have had myrrh within it.

Myrrh brings together the birth of Jesus and his death. It is a harsh reminder of what is going to happen. What might it have been like for Mary, with a new baby and all the hopes and excitement that brings, to be given a gift that would have spoken so clearly to her of death?

For us, the birth of Jesus is the beginning of his journey to the cross; a journey we know ends with resurrection. But for Mary it was another part in the jigsaw that told her that her baby was going to die, and that his life was already beginning to belong to others in ways she couldn't begin to imagine or understand.

Try spending some time holding the cross and the nativity together.

If you have a nativity set, try putting a cross within the scene. Or take a Christmas card showing the manger and draw a cross over it.

How does this feel? What are the joys and sadnesses this evokes?

What thoughts come to mind?

Along with the sadness of Good Friday, bring to mind the joy of Easter Day.

As a child

Phil Steer

Child

He called a little *child* and had him stand among them. (Matthew 18:2, NIV 1984, emphasis mine).

The disciples have just asked Jesus, 'Who is the greatest in the kingdom of heaven?' (or, more to the point, which of them is the greatest in the kingdom of heaven), and now they await his reply. There is, perhaps, just a hint of tension in the air, an uneasy truce at the end of all their squabbling. Soon they will have their answer; the argument will be settled once and for all. Some have reason to be quietly confident: Simon Peter, the 'rock' on whom Jesus would build his church (Matthew 16:18); James and John, the brothers who, with Peter, were granted a 'mountain-top experience', seeing Jesus transfigured and speaking with Moses and Elijah (Matthew 17:1–8). Others realise that they are probably not the front runners, but still feel that they are in with a chance: Andrew, Simon Peter's brother, who was the first to follow Jesus (John 1:35–42); Nathaniel, whom Jesus called 'a true Israelite' (v. 47); Judas, who has been entrusted with their money (13:29). The rest of the group wait more in hope than expectation; Thomas, especially, has his doubts.

There is, perhaps, a pause while Jesus appears to consider his reply, only adding to the tension and sense of anticipation. And then he calls forward a little child. Seemingly, Jesus hasn't heard their question. Or maybe he has chosen to ignore it? That would be just like him! So often in the past he has failed to give a straight answer to a perfectly straightforward question. Should they try asking again? And then Jesus speaks: 'Unless you change and become like little children, you will never enter the kingdom of heaven.' What was that? 'Never enter the kingdom of heaven'? Had they heard him correctly? Far from confirming their belief that they were near the top—if not at the top—of the spiritual pile, Jesus seems to be bringing into question whether they are even in the kingdom at all. And what was all this about becoming like little children? What on earth did that mean? How could they become like little children? And why would they want to?

You can almost hear their heads spinning as they try to get to grips with what Jesus has just said, and see their exchanged glances as they wonder which of them will be the first to voice the thoughts that are racing through their minds. But before they have a chance to say anything, Jesus continues: 'Therefore, whoever humbles himself like this child is the greatest in the kingdom of heaven' (Matthew 18:4).

What was this? The greatest in the kingdom of heaven was not Simon Peter or James or John, Jesus' closest companions; not another of the 'chosen Twelve', who had left everything to follow him; not one of Jesus' many other followers; not even one of the Pharisees or Sadducees or teachers of the law. No, the greatest in the kingdom of heaven was, apparently, anyone who humbled themselves like a little child.

By our usual criteria of greatness, this sounds like nonsense. How can a mere child possibly be great? Too young to have developed the abilities and skills and strengths that adults possess, what can a child possibly achieve? What position can they attain? What influence do they have? What authority can they be given? What power can they exercise? But all this is of no importance. A child is great in the kingdom of God for one reason above all others: because Jesus, the King of kings and Lord of lords, says that they are. Greatness in the kingdom is not something that can be attained through our own efforts and abilities, but rather something that is given by God. Just as the Roman Emperor could bestow greatness upon any that he chose to be part of his inner circle, so Jesus bestows greatness on those whom he calls closest to himself, on those who come to him like little children.

It is almost impossible for us to appreciate the full impact of Jesus' words on his disciples. We know full well what he was going to say, and so there is not the utter shock and surprise that they would have experienced on hearing his answer for the first time. But perhaps more than this, we also miss something of the reality—I might say the physicality—of Jesus' words. The disciples were not asking an abstract, theological question. They were expecting Jesus to bring about God's kingdom on earth, to 'restore the kingdom to Israel' (Acts 1:6), and they really wanted to know which of them would hold the positions of greatest honour and power. And Jesus didn't give them an abstract, theological answer. Rather, he called forward a little child—a real little child—and he said, if you want to be great in the kingdom of heaven, then *be like this*.

There is, I think, a tendency for us to understand Jesus' words to be simply an illustration, a metaphor of the need to have a childlike faith and a childlike trust in God. But to limit their meaning in this way is, I believe, to diminish the all-embracing, life-changing scope of what Jesus is actually asking of us. For the call to be childlike is one that has significance for each and every aspect of our daily lives.

Too many of us have lost touch with the child that we once were: left behind in our rush into the adult world, forgotten in our fascination with adult ways, banished for fear they might make us look foolish and neglected when it seemed they were no longer needed. Others, I know, will have been forced by circumstance to grow up far too quickly, never having had the opportunity truly to live as the child that God created you to be. As a consequence, we live our lives largely separated from our childlike self. But this is not the way we are meant to be. And so Jesus calls us to become like little children, to recover our childlike nature, and so discover the fullness of a kingdom that only the childlike can enter.

Spotlight: The Simeon Centre for Prayer and the Spiritual Life, Cambridge

Adrian Chatfield

The energy of a centre for prayer comes from a listening ear, an obedient heart and a driving passion to rediscover daily what it means to be friends with God and to help others who cross our threshold to do the same. Over the past five years, since our launch, this has been our constant focus.

Based uniquely in an Anglican theological college, the Simeon Centre for Prayer and the Spiritual Life has had a fourfold role:

- In caring for the personal and spiritual formation of the Ridley Hall community. This is a ministry gladly undertaken by all, students and staff, for each other. Discipleship is the responsibility of all, and the Centre is the catalyst for this work.
- In the academic teaching of spirituality and prayer within the Cambridge Theological Federation and more widely. Undergraduate modules, dissertation and thesis supervision, invitational events and periodic conferences all contribute towards this part of our ministry.

- In resourcing the wider church through offering spiritual direction, particularly to church leaders; through responding to requests for training and consultancy; and by leading, chaplaining and speaking at conferences, retreats and other events.
- In working with others across a range of networks, raising the profile of Christian perspectives in the public square and in the churches. We have held conferences on 'dying well' and on spirituality and dementia, and worked with partner organisations and individuals on marriage, singleness and gender imbalance in our churches, the ethics of human enhancement and men's spirituality.

The last item hints at the underlying questions that remain at the heart of our vocation and our spiritual quest. We are creaturely beings, made in the image and likeness of a sovereign God, who calls us in love to stand before his majesty, to sit and feast with him, and to work towards the coming of his kingdom.

In order to do this faithfully and well, we need to understand and engage with what it means to be human. In our contemporary contexts, how do we balance our understanding of disability with our hunger for drug and genetic enhancement? How, too, can we learn to value individuals as they are, while believing that God longs for them to be redeemed, more fulfilled in themselves and in life, and complete in Christ? And in relation to the way in which we do church, can we resist the temptation to gather like with like, so that the diversity and complexity of God's created order is not compromised?

Strangely, then, we have found ourselves—as a Centre for Prayer—spending much time in busy thought, reflecting on our humanity, believing that when we know ourselves fully as we are known by God, the relationship that we enjoy with him is restored, strengthened and nurtured.

To be human in a proper sense is, first and foremost, about gift: the gift of life, if you will. We believe that life is given by God who breathes life into us; and we are born again—redeemed—through the self-giving Son of God. As inheritors of the kingdom of heaven, we are given the Holy Spirit as a guarantee, another kind of gift. Even the world that we inhabit is gifted to us for our care and stewardship.

Solidarity comes a close second. There are as many theories about being made in God's image and likeness as there are theologians, but my take on it depends on the implicit 'we' in Genesis 1. The nature of God is not plural but relational. The three persons of the one God dwell in mutual love, harmony and interdependent purpose. And it is 'we' who are made in that image, and reflect it only in community, only in relationship with one another, only as 'one people', only in mutuality and sharing.

It naturally flows from this that the virtues proper to being human, apart from the cardinal virtue of love, are those of companionship, hospitality, compassion, humility, vulnerability and reconciliation. If we live life in gratitude for its giftedness and in communion with one another, all relationships flourish, most notably our relationship with God. And since prayer is not a task, a duty or a work, but the language of a primary relationship, our praying will find its tongue when we are true to our common humanity under God.

To find out more about the Centre or issues raised in this article, please email the administrator, Rosemary Kew, at rak44@cam.ac.uk, ring Adrian Chatfield on 01223 746590, or go to the website at www.simeoncentre. co.uk

Quiet Spaces Subscription

Prices are correct May 2013–April 2014.

Please note one-year subscription prices below include postage and packing.

You can also purchase your subcription by Direct Debit. Complete the details on the direct debit form and post to BRF with the order form.

Please send *Quiet Spaces* beginning with the January 2014/May 2014/ September 2014 issue (delete as applicable).

PRICES FOR UK ADDRESSES

DESCRIPTION	PRICE	QUANTITY ORDERED	TOTAL
Individual 1-year subscription Includes postage and packing	£15.00		
Group 1-year subscription Postage and packing FREE	£12.00		
ORDER TOTAL			

PRICES FOR OVERSEAS ADDRESSES

DESCRIPTION	PRICE	QUANTITY ORDERED	TOTAL
Individual 1-year subscription Airmail includes postage and packing	£24.00		
Individual 1-year subscription Surface includes postage and packing	£21.60		
Group 1-year subscription Postage and packing FREE	£16.50		
ORDER TOTAL			

Method of payment

☐ Cheque ☐ MasterCard ☐ Maestro ☐ Visa ☐ Postal Order

Card no. ☐☐☐☐ ☐☐☐☐ ☐☐☐☐ ☐☐☐☐ ☐☐☐

Shaded boxes for Maestro use only

Valid from ☐☐ ☐☐   Expires ☐☐ ☐☐   Issue No.
(Switch only) ☐☐☐☐

Security code* ☐☐☐ (Last 3 digits on the reverse of the card)   *0000* **000**
Essential in order to process your order   EXAMPLE

Signature .... Date ...... / ...... / ....

All subscription orders must be accompanied by the appropriate payment.

Please note: do not send payments for group orders. All group orders will be invoiced.

Name ....

Acc. No. ....

Address ....

....

.... Postcode ....

Telephone ....

Email ....

BRF, 15 The Chambers, Vineyard, Abingdon OX14 3FE;
Tel: 01865 319700 Fax: 01865 319701
www.brf.org.uk email: enquiries@brf.org.uk
BRF is a registered charity (no: 233280)

BRF Quiet Days

BRF Quiet Days are an ideal way of redressing the balance in our busy lives. Held in peaceful locations around the country, each one is led by an experienced speaker and gives the opportunity to reflect, be silent and pray, and through it all to draw closer to God.

The remaining days in the 2013 programme are as follows:

Tuesday 24 September: 'Praying with Henri Nouwen' led by Sally Smith at The Chapter House, St Mary-in-Charnwood, Nanpanton, Leicestershire.

Thursday 21 November: 'Pilgrimage' led by Sally Welch at The Harnhill Centre of Christian Healing, Harnhill Manor, Gloucestershire.

Wednesday 4 December: 'The Coming of God' led by Ann Persson at a venue in south Oxfordshire tbc.

For further details and to book please go to www.brfonline.org.uk/events-and-quiet-days or contact us at BRF, 15 The Chambers, Vineyard, Abingdon, Oxfordshire, OX14 3FE; tel: 01865 319700

Direct Debit

Now you can pay for your annual subscription to BRF notes using Direct Debit. You need only give your bank details once, and the payment is made automatically every year until you cancel it. If you would like to pay by Direct Debit, please use the form opposite, entering your BRF account number under 'Reference'.

You are fully covered by the Direct Debit Guarantee:

The Direct Debit Guarantee

- This Guarantee is offered by all banks and building societies that accept instructions to pay Direct Debits.
- If there are any changes to the amount, date or frequency of your Direct Debit, The Bible Reading Fellowship will notify you 10 working days in advance of your account being debited or as otherwise agreed. If you request The Bible Reading Fellowship to collect a payment, confirmation of the amount and date will be given to you at the time of the request.
- If an error is made in the payment of your Direct Debit, by The Bible Reading Fellowship or your bank or building society, you are entitled to a full and immediate refund of the amount paid from your bank or building society.
  - If you receive a refund you are not entitled to, you must pay it back when The Bible Reading Fellowship asks you to.
- You can cancel a Direct Debit at any time by simply contacting your bank or building society. Written confirmation may be required. Please also notify us.

The Bible Reading Fellowship

Instruction to your bank or building society to pay by Direct Debit

DIRECT Debit

Please fill in the whole form using a ballpoint pen and send to The Bible Reading Fellowship, 15 The Chambers, Vineyard, Abingdon OX14 3FE.

Service User Number: | 5 | 5 | 8 | 2 | 2 | 9 |

Name and full postal address of your bank or building society

To: The Manager ....

.... Bank/Building Society

Address ....

....

.... Postcode ....

Name(s) of account holder(s)

Branch sort code

☐☐ – ☐☐ – ☐☐

Bank/Building Society account no.

☐☐☐☐☐☐☐☐

Reference

☐☐☐☐☐☐

Instruction to your Bank/Building Society

Please pay The Bible Reading Fellowship Direct Debits from the account detailed in this instruction, subject to the safeguards assured by the Direct Debit Guarantee. I understand that this instruction may remain with The Bible Reading Fellowship and, if so, details will be passed electronically to my bank/building society.

Signature(s)

Date

Banks and Building Societies may not accept Direct Debit instructions for some types of account.